i will love you for evermore

Copyright © 2023 Amiee Knubley

All rights reserved. This book or parts thereof may not be reproduced in any form, stored in any retrieval system, or transmitted in any form by any means—electronic, mechanical, photocopy, recording, or otherwise—without prior written permission of the publisher. For permission requests, write to the publisher Luna Love & Co (Amiee Knubley).

ISBN 978-0-6454964-5-1 (Paperback)

Portions of this book are works of fiction. Any references to historical events, real people, or real places are used fictitiously. Other names, characters, places and events are products of the author's imagination, and any resemblances to actual events or places or persons, living or dead, is entirely coincidental.

Artwork by Amiee Knubley.

First printing edition 2023.

Luna Love & Co
South Australia

ABN 72 373 179 282

i will love you for evermore

PREFACE	7
CHAPTER ONE – FALLING IN LOVE	**11**
WISH FULFILMENT	15
FATES RULE	16
MOVING FORWARD	17
TWIN FLAME	18
THE RAIN	20
HEALING LOVE	22
LOVE	24
THOUGHTS BEFORE SLEEP	27
MORE THAN LOVE	28
THE WAIT	30
IF WE LET IT	32
MY SECRET	35
FOREVER	36
I LOVE YOU MORE	38
PROMISE	39
PROUD	40
HOME	41
UNCONDITIONAL	42
EVERMORE	43
MEANT TO	44
SILENT LOVE	45
REGRET	46
CHASER	47
FATE	48
ALWAYS	49
FEAR OF IT ALL	50
DESTINY	51
THE WAY I DO	52
FOR REAL	54
LOVING YOU	56
STRANGERS	57
CHAPTER TWO – HEARTBREAK	**59**
YOUR VOICE	62
HISTORY	64
IT WAS MAGIC	65
GONE	66
THE SADDEST GOODBYE	67
YOUR HEART	68
SILENCE	70
DARE TO	71

LOVERS PASSED	72
LIAR	73
NORTH STAR	74
BEFORE YOU	76
LETS NOT SAY GOODBYE	79
I WILL MISS YOU	80
THANK YOU MY OLD FRIEND	83
VICTIMLESS	84
NEVER AGAIN	85
LIGHT	86
BLACK AND WHITE	87
GOODBYE	88
LIES	89
SORRY	90
THE SEPARATION	92

CHAPTER THREE – MOTHERHOOD   **95**

MOTHER ENOUGH	98
I PROMISE	99
MY SON	100
HER	102
DEAR HEART	104
MY WISH FOR YOU	105
LA LUNE	106
MISCARRIAGE	107
INFERTILITY	108
GRIEF	109
APRIL 4TH	110
HOPE	112
LOSS	115
INFERTILE PROMISE	116
GREEN	118
JUNE 19TH	120
PHEONIX	122
FOR LUNA	124
MOTHERHOOD	127

CHAPTER FOUR – SELF   **129**

TOMORROW	132
PERFECTLY DESIGNED	133
LONLINESS	134
THE UNIVERSE	135

FAITHS CALLING	136
IT'S OK	138
LOVE YOURSELF FIRST	139
MY HOME	140
WHAT NOW?	142
INTUITION	143
BLESSINGS	144
HOW LONG?	145
WAR	146
UNCOMFORTABLE PEACE	147
MY BROKEN HEART	148
THE FIGHT	149
TOO FAR	151
FOR YOU	152
I LOVE ME TOO	154
YOU ARE EVERYTHING	156
THE LITTLE THINGS	157
YOU ARE THE LIGHT	158
SOULMATE	159
ANYTHING LESS	160
ENGLISH BAY	162
NO	163
SELF BELIEF	164
HEALER	167
END	**168**
JOURNAL	**171**

'EVERMORE'

-

*For those who taught me what love should be, and
for those who taught me what love should never be
- I will remember you, always, forever,
for evermore...*

i will love you for evermore

PREFACE

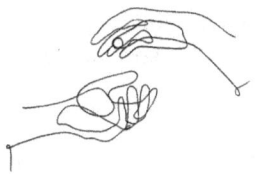

This book contains all of the untold poetry and letters about the love in my life, split into chapters and collections - in almost a way of compartmentalising my heart. This collection spans years of my written work through self-discovery in my early twenties, learning how to love, the desperation of infertility and loss, grief, separation, and heartbreak but also the most magical experiences of all, true love, motherhood, friendship, and self-acceptance. The poetry and letters written are from my heart, honest and vulnerable and some to a lover that I never shared. Some are letters written to myself, for myself, and messages I have received in the truest form of guidance I ever needed - my spiritual connection.

Not all love in my life has resulted in pain, some is the product of it, pure gritty and raw love created in the moments in life where courage and strength are the only pillars to survive. What I can say, and what I can promise of love, is that no matter what other story surrounds it, be it motherhood, friendship, heartbreak, or oneself; every love has a moment of unexplainable joy. Be it fleeting or long lasting, it is a moment where your skin is alive with an energy of fireworks but also contentedness and a knowing that exists at the same time. This is what our energy is made for. Our existence. Our being. It all comes down to these moments. These moments where we feel most alive.

Poetry and letter writing is an art form which has immense power. The power to put exactly how we, and maybe how another human being, is feeling into words. To communicate the unexplainable.

To connect with those who cannot fathom how similar all of our experiences are. To allow us to feel. Like most, I've seen a lot in my life, lived through a lot of joy and pain. Not only survived, but I have thrived. What I have learned, is that through it all we have a choice, and when the time calls for it, we must choose to feel it so that we can experience the life meant for us, to heal.

We must choose to feel the happiness when it is here because around the corner may be something else entirely. When the pain comes, we must choose to feel that too, but we must not get stuck there, because there is always light in the darkness, always.

I hope that whatever you are searching for, you will find inbetween my words held within, and when you do, you find pieces of yourself that you have lost along the way. I hope that in this you may be able to understand or explain your story, and maybe that is one that has to date, remained untold. As you read I encourage you to write in the margins, highlight words or sentences that speak to you, and use the space at the end of the book to begin emptying your heart.

I pray that you feel courageous enough to share your voice, and your experience, because that vulnerability may just connect you to the light that was always there. The light that you need to find. Please remember that no one situation defines you, and with no clarifiers or caveats, please know that you are important in this world.

What you do matters.

You are loved, more than you could ever know; and you are enough, just as you are. With all of the broken, all of the beautiful and messy raw truth you hold, *you are enough.*

All my love,
Always, forever, for evermore.
Amiee

i will love you for evermore

Amiee Laura Knubley

CHAPTER ONE

falling in love
-

I use the term *falling* to describe the collection of poems and love letters in this chapter because it is the only physical sensation which actually describes the feeling for me. A supernatural and illogical experience. I don't think we step into love with a plan, a reliable list and all the tools we need - we fall (sometimes slow and sometimes fast) and for many, the experience is chaotic and uncertain. Yes magical, but as humans we don't have all of the answers, and that makes it hard. We cannot see how it will, or if it will, happen. I can't help but think that this is the way it is exactly meant to be. So that we actually let go and allow another soul to completely take over our rational minds momentarily to allow them into our beautiful and messy lives, for as long, as well, they are meant to stay.

This collection is created to guide you through the spectrum of emotions that falling in love makes us feel. From the hopeful, to the sure and steady, to the desperation and the hopelessness we can often find ourselves in . That will be found and expressed in poems like *'twin flame'*. The hopeless romantic in me wants falling in love to be like the movies, to be flowers and sunsets and all the right words at the right times. But it's not. It doesn't happen in a straight line and it doesn't always happen the way we picture; and looking back, isn't that the best part of the story?

Poems like *'wish fulfilment'* are written from a place of hope and anticipation, and I hope that after reading you are taken to a place where you are reminded of, or are shown a light you may not have felt before. Reminiscent of the expectant, the desire and the openness of the new stages love. Comparing this to the chaotic and almost self sabotage tactics we can play when we are afraid, simply for no other reason than because we feel.

Falling in love can feel like a comedy show and *'soulmate'* was written to incite a smile, but really the epitome of falling will be found in the likes of *'forever'* and *'evermore'*. If you haven't felt a love like this before, I hope you do, because in one single moment it set my soul on fire and healed every part of me.

There is no right way to fall in love, but a good place to start is to let yourself feel. Each and everyone one of us is worthy of love, one that is consistent and safe, but exciting and hopeful. One where each other is heard, is seen, and is respected. We aren't meant to do this life alone and falling in love is a blessing that we get to experience in our lives. For some it happens many times over until one day we meet our person. The person that makes us better, makes us choose life, and supports us as we say yes to all of the beautiful and messy parts we get to live for.

I pray this collection takes you somewhere and gives you exactly what you need.

All my love,
Always, forever, for evermore,
Amiee

i will love you for evermore

i will love you for evermore

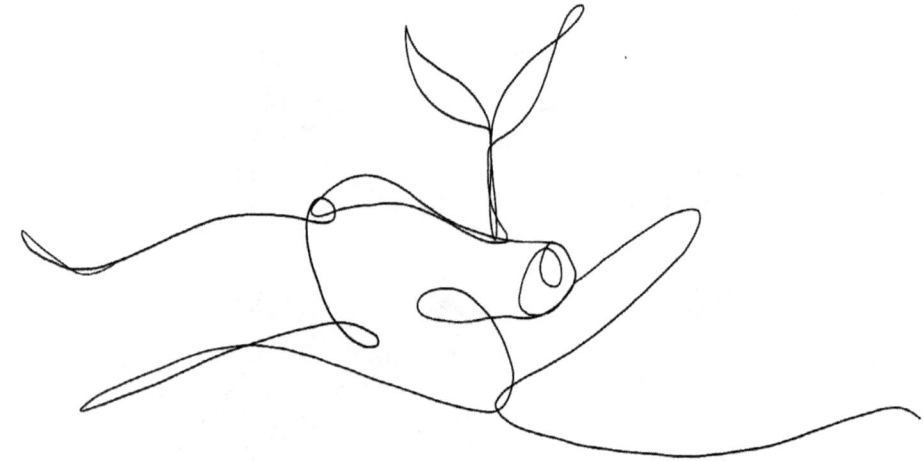

i will love you for evermore

God, Universe, Spirits, I *know* you hear me,
and for a moment I hope you'll indulge me as I
    dream a little selfishly.
I've never been more ready.
I've done the work and I've healed the broken parts
    that felt a bit *unsteady.*

I worry about time,
and maybe that I've treated love *before*
    like a throwaway dime.
But I understand now.
I know you have a plan and I don't get to know the how.
But can I ask one thing?
About this love that you are *about* to bring.

That he is kind and makes choices with *abundant generosity.*
That he is patient and always a little bit funny.
With a curious mind, he will be open to hear it all,
but he will be stable so he can catch me *when I fall.*
He will value family and he will create safety,
because he will know
    that's the foundation that our life has to be.
From there he will *want to grow,*
because he knows his purpose and those are the seeds
                    that he will sow.

I'm not sure what he will believe.
But he'll know of faith and just like me, he won't give to receive,
because he's lived a life seeing that there is *always more,*
and we can always be better if we just open the door.

Thank you for listening,
and working out *this* blessing.
I promise to be me,
and exactly the light you've guided me to be.

    - wish fufilment

Amiee Laura Knubley

What is meant for you never truly leaves.
It is this we can rely, *the only rule that guarantees.*

- fates rule

MOVING FORWARD

Waiting is never forever, this I know,
but this doesn't feel like magic, like the wait for falling snow.
This feels hopeless, like waiting for the rain to stop,
an unbalanced in-between of never reaching the top.

   I ask out-loud *"what should I do?"*,
to the universe and to anyone who's invested in this too.
But the answers are always the same,
   *"you have to take it slow and no you can't go back the
                     way you came"*.

You see, I can't unknow you and given the chance,
   I wouldn't.
You're in my heart forever, in ways a person shouldn't.
My skin knows your voice
           and the way your words move *together*.
I can predict the falling sounds in the same way an anchor, is
   a *boats tether*.

I know waiting isn't forever and soon enough I'll know,
but I pray the answer comes
                   before the tide becomes too low.

i will love you for evermore

We could have the rest of our lives together
so what's a few more
    months of this *agonising wait?*
I hope we have an infinity of tomorrows,
    a love that's built on fate.

This neither here nor there *lights up my anxiety,*
    but that's not who I want to be.

I don't want to wait because I think about all the
    things to be done.
Why would I want to wait, when you,
    my love, are my sun.

       - twin flame

i will love you for evermore

Amiee Laura Knubley

i will love you for evermore

THE RAIN

A million times I can say it.
The words never seem to fit.
Like the rain is falling too slow,
over a silence we wouldn't know.

Pick your time, your clever line.
Just please don't say you're fine,
when really your skin is on fire.
Your eyes, always becoming the liar.

Your stars are always changing,
to a darkness so blinding.
Together but a light,
apart a lonely sight.

Don't you crave the light.
My heart, my peace, or even just my sight?
I can't make you hear me.
Just don't close your eyes to see.

Darling, it's your dice to roll.
Time against your soul.
A beating drum, singing your song,
of where your heart belongs.

The path *will* show.
This I *know*.
So, a million times I will say it,
    because one day the words will fit.

i will love you for evermore

Amiee Laura Knubley

i will love you for evermore

Dear you,

As you sit there in your wonderful strength, I want to say that I am proud of you. I am proud of you for keeping your heart open. After what has happened in your life, you could have easily decided that this part of you would be shut away for good. No-one would have judged you or even questioned you for a moment, if you chose a path of yourself; without love.

That isn't a choice you have made though. Your heart is open and in your light others are drawn to you. People are drawn to your warm energy, your kindess, your strength. They want to follow because they know if they do, they will see the magic that life is offering.

As you sit there in your inspiring curiosity, I am in awe of you. I am in awe of how even after it all you stand not because of what happened to you, but despite what happened to you. You see that there is good in the world, there is good that is pure and surrounded by light and the darkness was only where you were for a time. I am in awe of how you still truely trust that abundant, fufilling and pure love is meant for you, is meant for us all.

You sit there open, authenic and warm, ready for what is to come. You are ready to bring all the versions of you, knowing that true love will see you, will hear you and will accept you just as you are. You know you wont have to fight, chase and prove to love that you are worthy - love will already know. You know that you wont have to run from, question or doubt love becuase love will provide consistency, safety and knowing.

As I sit here and I think about all of the moments in life that have brought you to today, I beam with pride. When you were afraid, you felt it but still found courage. When you were lost, you rested for a while but still moved forward into the unknown.

i will love you for evermore

When you were burdened with grief you let it take you whole, knowing that was part of the process and you would emerge new, with grief being a strong pillar that would be a part of you forever. When you felt joy, you were present and you stayed with it for as long as you could becuase you knew its real blessing. When you were needed you arrived and you stayed for as long as you were called for.

When you were abandoned, used and tormented you fell down forgetting your power but you chose to do the work to heal becuase you are not what happened to you.

Knowing all of this about you fills me with immense joy at the thought of the love that is coming for you. A soul that matches yours is going to be pure magic for they will be made from the same as you. You will stand and eye to eye, see each other for your before, for your now and for your tomorrows.

I know that when this love comes, that whilst you will not run, you will cry. You will cry from relief that you have been found and in that moment I hope you realise that you no longer have to do this alone anymore.

You will have found your strength in another who will walk through the fire with you. You will have found your peace in another who will sit with you and feel the light that surrounds you. You will have found your curosity in another who will always wonder and will always find the answers with you. You will have found your drive in another who will take each step with you as you keep moving forward.

As you sit there in your wonderful strength, again I want to say that I am proud of you.

Always,
Me   *- healing love*

i will love you for evermore

I wouldn't change it,
because then I wouldn't be standing here in front of you.
Hindsight is a wonderful thing because now
   I know it was those steps I had to do.

But I wonder did I really have to travel
   across the world for our paths to collide?
Was my miscarriage a necessary *low tide.*
Those nights I sat in darkness if I had the choice,
   I probably wouldn't keep,
but I guess surviving that, gave me the courage,
   to take the leap.

A decade of endless winters in my mind,
gave me the hope I probably wouldn't otherwise find.
I emerged a fighter, with a soul made from loss,
like the most beautiful flower *hidden*
   ever so slightly under a green moss.

You see, slowly I grew,
becoming a light through and through.
Like a lighthouse in the night,
showing others how to win *this* fight.

That's when you saw me.
A picture of everything I had been before
   and everything I would be.
So would I change it?
No. Not at all,
   how could I risk missing the best bit.

   - *love*

i will love you for evermore

i will love you for evermore

i will love you for evermore

Am I the last thing on your mind,
because you are the first on mine.
Do you dream of me,
    or is it another that you see?
I wake to your name on my tongue,
words unspoken, a song unsung.
I don't think you see how amazing you are.
You definitely don't feel the strength that's got you
                      this far.

    - thoughts before sleep

i will love you for evermore

Dear you,

I love you with a love that's more than love. I'll never say these words outloud so this letter will have to do.

I open my eyes and your smile is still there, an air of hope in this life I haven't felt before. Like the sun as it rises and like the moon as it shines. In every moment I think if how you are. I wonder if you are you proud of the choices you are making, whether you felt the light today or if you heard a song that described exactly as you felt? I did. I so wanted to tell you, *but I didn't.*

I love you with a love that's more than love. In the never, I long for your hand to touch mine, for you to kiss my neck, to hear your laugh, tell me about your day, watch my name on your tongue; setting my skin on fire. Every hair on edge as you look into my eyes.

We've met before. Not in this life time but in everyone before. Our souls an exact match. A story of a thousand lives where in each we find each other.

I love you with a love that's more than love. You are home to me. I knew from the moment I heard you say my name, from the moment you looked into my eyes. You are my safety, my joy, my peace, my thrill.

I know that I am the same for you, so take your time my love. I'll be here waiting, in this life and the next. Because I love you with a love that's more than love. I know its crazy, and it's why I'll never speak it.

I've never felt a love like this.

Always,
Me

                    - more than love

Amiee Laura Knubley

i will love you for evermore

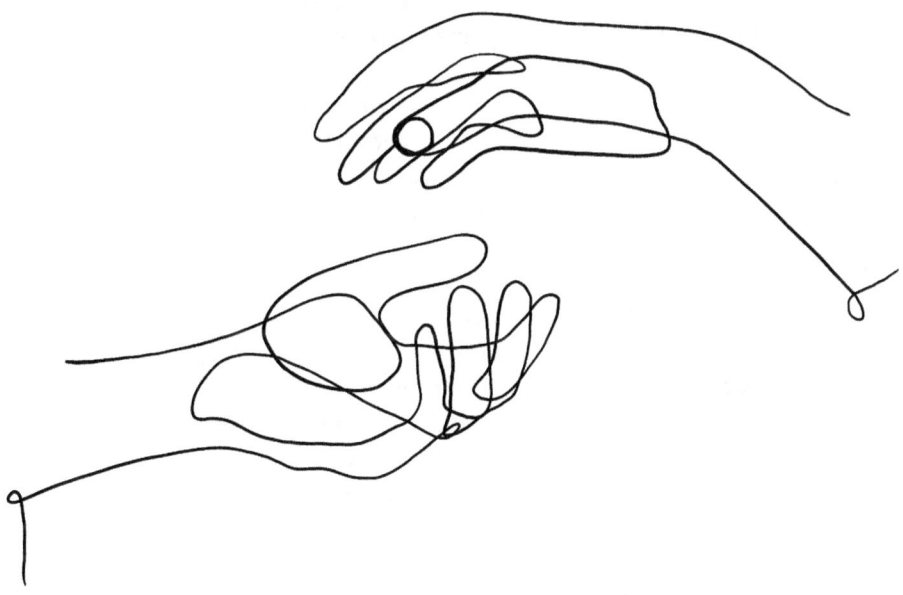

Amiee Laura Knubley

i will love you for evermore

THE WAIT

I am all or nothing but with you I am
    in this complicated in-between.
I would give you everything the moment you said.
I would give you a love you've never had,
  a life where all your past moments have led.

I knew the moment I met you that we had done
  this dance before.
Our souls connected at the core.
I will give you a love that will rebuild your heart.
I promise it will be easy and *not a fine art.*

Good morning messages and stories to make you laugh.
Dreams and wishes together so nothing is done in half.
Love letters, surprise gifts, *flowers*,
mini adventures and dances in the garden
    when it *showers.*

Music for stolen moments.
Everyday a life well spent.
Breakfast in bed and coffee *I love yous.*
You will be my best friend, my inspiration, *my muse.*
I will hold you and kiss you in every moment I can,
  because I will be your biggest fan.

I will hold your hand as you walk in the fire,
and I will catch you every time that you tire.
You will have my heart in *whatever way you need,*
and I will let you carry it, as I carry yours
    wherever our feet lead.

Amiee Laura Knubley

i will love you for evermore

For my love is forever.
For the midnight dances and a love so tender.
For the sea escapes,
              and the cheesy mixtapes.
For the dark and the messy and when everything
   seems too hard,
I will be there, your gentle and *unwavering* life guard.

My love for you, *when you are ready*, will be forever.
Not just a maybe, it's a life changing surrender.
But for now I know, your heart is heavy, you're frozen
       in the before, in the unsteady.

So, I will hold back this love, following your lead.
Until you find me, until you say that you are ready,
   Until you say that I am all you will ever need.

Amiee Laura Knubley

i will love you for evermore

IF WE LET IT

Why did you close your eyes when I said it out loud.
The air left my lungs and my feet no longer stood proud.
Those seconds waiting felt like a lifetime
Like I was waiting for the judge to sentence my biggest
                                              crime.

Why do I cry when you hold me as gently as you do.
I know it wasn't a lie when you said you felt it too.
You caught me when the wind left me.
And in this moment we both knew.

This was it.
A moment we would never forget, *not even a little bit.*
I found you and you found me.
This, the start of the greatest love story *ever to be.*

i will love you for evermore

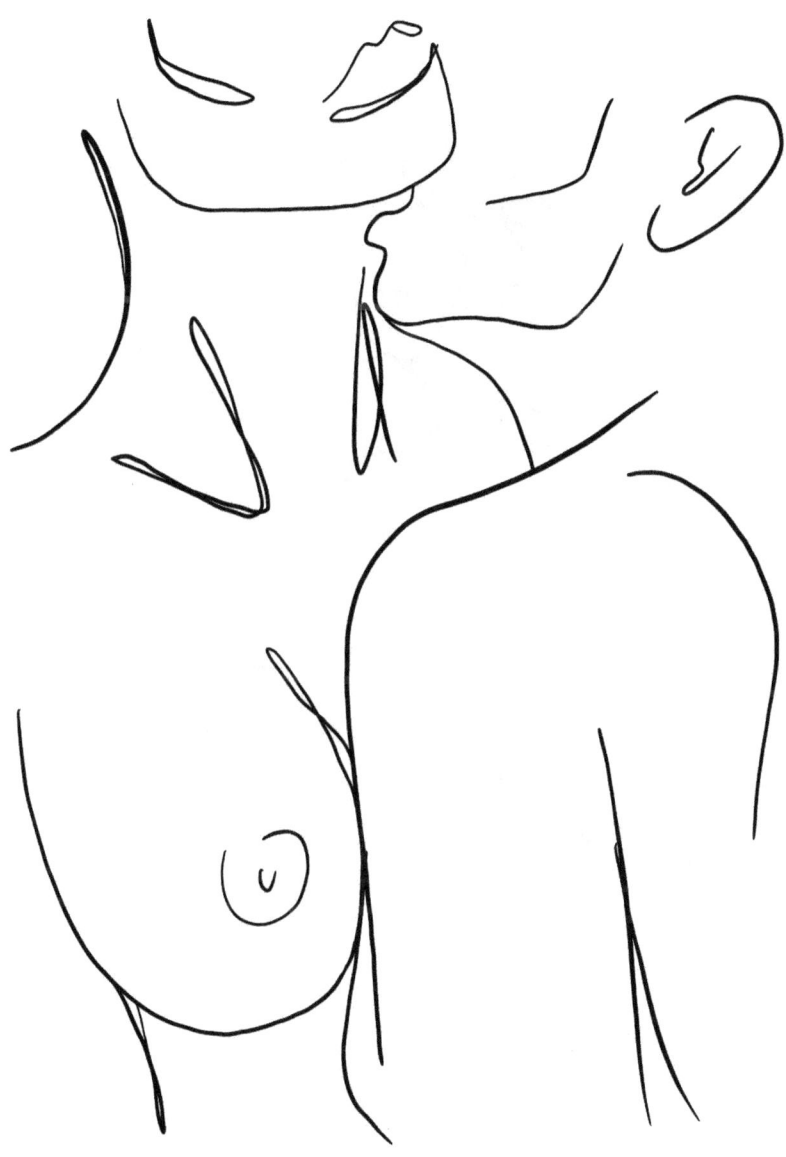

i will love you for evermore

Amiee Laura Knubley

i will love you for evermore

Can I tell you my biggest secret?
If I say it, please promise *you* will keep it…

You are the song I have been missing,
and in my heart we are always kissing.

- my secret

FOREVER

I wish you could see yourself through my eyes, and not through your doubt, your hurt or through all the lies. Because you are the finest, the loveliest and most tender person *I have met*. Your eyes steal all my words and your smile starts the bet.

You are built with a strength made of courage and deep love. Because you see each person and every piece they are made of. You look at things from every angle possible, and when you've decided, your mind is simply unchangeable.

Your vulnerability is rare. But the way you create space can sometimes be too much to bare. I wish you knew you weren't alone. Your independence isn't the best badge that you own.

Your thoughts are magic with the way they hold the world together. You breathe out colour and you dance *as if you've known forever.* I'm so bloody glad you exist, and I knew that, *before we first kissed.*

You are important, *yes to me,* but to everyone you meet. You don't see it, but you are made from a fire, a light *and you never miss a beat.* You shine like a firefly at night, with the way you dream and plan with all your might.

Your face is beautiful, and *yes I see the hidden scars,* holding all the pain like you don't deserve the stars. Your laugh makes me feel at home, and that our souls no longer need to roam.

I wish you could see yourself through my eyes, because I'm in awe of you *and I promise my love will not be one that dies.*

i will love you for evermore

Amiee Laura Knubley

i will love you for evermore

Dear you,

I love you.

I love the way that you see the world and how you choose light in your life despite it all. I admire your strength and how you have chosen courage.

You are an amazing human and I am so lucky to have you in my life. I love the way your voice changes and as you get more passionate you become more pronounced. Your eyes make me lose myself. I love how you squint when you laugh, and how you roll your eyes at me.

Your words can heal. Yours tell the stories of love and heartbreak and I love the way I can see your soul grows after each one.

I miss you when I'm not talking to you and I want you to be by my side always. Holding you feels like home and I have never felt more alive, or safer.

You are amazing and everyday *I will love you more.*

Aways,
Me

  - i love you more

i will love you for evermore

Forever only happens when you show up everyday.
You keep your word and mean what you say.
Can you carry me when I fall?
It's the only way this works, taking it in turns
giving our all.

Doing what we can,
when *nothing* follows our plan.
Keeping our eyes on each other,
because otherwise, *why bother?*

- *promise*

PROUD

You sent me a photo of a cloud,
and I sat there smiling, feeling immensely *proud*.
You saw a moment of joy and you stopped
    to capture the magic.
I hope now it's a favourite memory that you will pick.

Not because of the cloud or the red sky behind it,
but for the moment you made a choice *to just sit.*
You smiled at where you were
    and you choose to share it.
I hope now you keep your eyes open,
        even just a little bit.

i will love you for evermore

HOME

You don't have to hold back tears,
                because I am right here.
Some stories are worth telling,
and ours I am not short selling.
Our story had me homebound,
because *the day I fell for you*
                was the day I was found.

Amiee Laura Knubley

UNCONDITIONAL

Tell me what you are running from.
I'm worried this is what you will become.
Tell me why you can't look me in the eye.
I promise I will hold you through every cry.

Not everyone will hurt you.
There are people in the world who have good to do.
    People like me,
and how I wish this was a truth you could see.

The choice is yours and only one for you,
to believe so you can see the beauty in people too.
Isn't it lonely putting up that wall?
Those bricks will be your biggest down fall.

Tell me what you are running from.
Let me help you not feel so numb.
Together makes it a little easier to heal.
I promise I am here, no matter what it is that you feel.

i will love you for evermore

EVERMORE

Give me your broken.
Give me all your words you've left unspoken,
and I will carry them for you,
because I will give you strength and the reminder of
    everything you can do.

Give me your heartbreak.
Give me the shame you didn't need to take,
and I will carry it for you,
because I will love you, even when you remember how
  to do that too.

Give me your tears.
Give me all the battles you've lost over the years,
and I will stand here with you,
because you shouldn't do this alone but you know this,
    I know you do.

You've heard me and I've always heard you.
Now can we do this together too?
Because I promise, my love for you is an
  unbreakable tether.
  It is evermore, it is always and forever.

Amiee Laura Knubley

i will love you for evermore

MEANT TO

What is meant for me will stay.
But I can feel you slipping away.
Trust the path I'm on they cry,
but I wonder what magic could come after *this high*.

You are gentle like I had dreamed.
Your words more beautiful than they seemed.
Your heart matches mine,
our minds a woven parallel line.

If what is meant for me will stay.
Then why are you slipping away.
What will be, will be,
I just hope that it is you and me.

i will love you for evermore

I miss you.
I miss hearing your voice,
your silly laugh and how you say my name.
I miss seeing you smile.

I can't tell you this though
because you told me you can't love me,
but now that is all I can do.

You see all I can do is love you.
So, I will do that in the silence.
I'll love you from right here.

   - silent love

i will love you for evermore

If I was standing at your door,
tears rolling down my face asking for more.
What would you do?
Would that be the moment you finally knew?

I'd run a red light to get to you in time.
I'd give it my all and surrender like its my biggest crime.
If that would make you stay.
If it would feel easier that way.
I would love you like that.
Forgetting myself with each and every bat.

- regret

i will love you for evermore

CHASER

We've done this dance before.
In a different lifetime, in another world,
    I'm certain of it, I'm sure.
I can feel when you're thinking about me,
even from here *I can feel your energy.*
It sounds crazy, believe me, I know,
    but I'm not the one running this show.

I think in the life before I was a runner
    always filled with fear.
You were the stable heart
    who could never quite get near.
But in this life, I have learned the lessons I needed to,
so if you can't find me this time,
    just know in the next one,
        I won't run from you.

Amiee Laura Knubley

i will love you for evermore

I believe in *you*,
and all the magic you can do.
Your strength, your love, your song,
it will take you to where you belong.

I see *you*,
and everything you can do.
A fire inside that is burning so bright.
You are filling the world with your light.

Hold on to *me*,
when there is no path to see.
Life led you to this,
a moment with me you *cannot* miss.

I believe in *you*.
I see you.
So, now just hold on to me,
and let's see what will be.

   - fate

i will love you for evermore

ALWAYS

Have you felt the *'I can't live without you love'?*
Until you, I hadn't,
    but now it's the only phrase I can think of.
I've felt the love that sets your skin on fire,
    but once that fades there is nothing left to admire.

I've felt the love where you live to just fix them,
    like a beautiful dress that always has a ripped hem.
I've felt the love where they feel like your sun,
but it is so intense that after a while you can't help but
    need *to be done.*

The fire feels too much but also not enough.
Throughout all these I've craved the perfect balance
               but finding that is, *tough.*
I think the *'I can't live without you love'*
    feels like you are finally yourself.

Like the moment a butterfly feels their wings
    for the first time.
You're a little unsteady
    but with each flutter you can't help but shine.
It feels like the first day of spring.
When the sun warms your face
              and the birds begin to sing.

Like the night before Christmas
    when the snow begins to fall.
You sit and smile knowing there is only one person
              you want to call.
I think of *this type of love now*, because we got so close
    to feeling and knowing how.

Amiee Laura Knubley

i will love you for evermore

You pierce my soul and I am half agony, half hope,
but I know that if I had the courage to begin down this slope,
the wind would be in my hair and I would be coming for you.
Instead I'm just too scared to tell you that I, love you too.

I'm like an almost lover, frozen in time,
    like the moment before sunrise,
where the orange guides the bird away as it flies.
Does holding onto hope make me mad?
Because I feel wonderfully insane and *only a quarter bit sad.*

It's like I'm chasing a speeding racer by walking
And my feet are crumbling away *as I am talking.*
Holding onto hope is wishfully romantic, I know.
And I wish I wasn't born with enough love to fuel
    a Shakespearian show.

You know I would be no Juliette here.
I would be backstage *filled with fear.*
And you alone would take centre stage,
reciting the words off of every beautiful page.

The audience would love you of course,
and tears would fall as you rode away on your horse.
They would all fall in love with a story so sad.
    The tale of us and the *chance we never had.*

- fear of it all

i will love you for evermore

Maybe this is how it is meant to be.
Separated and never to see.
Even though he felt like home within,
and she set his heart on the biggest spin.

They saw each other in *every* moment,
but life had made them as each others opponent.
He set her body on fire at just a single thought.
And she was like a dream, he never could have caught.

But they found each other.
There could never be another.

Life kept them apart.
Two bodies, two souls but always one heart.
Right now, maybe that's meant to be,
but they will find each other, *just you wait and see.*

-destiny

THE WAY I DO

I love too much, too hard, too fast.
Holding my heart on a flag, like a giant welcome mast.
I show my cards too soon.
A chronic over-thinker, guided by the brightest moon.

I won't ever stop this part of me,
Because one day I will stand in front of him,
    and he will see.
Him, being the one I travelled life times for.
The one who didn't need me to open the door.

He will see me in the dark and he won't need a map.
There will be no silence, no wondering,
    no unachievable gap.
He'll love my weird stories and the way I talk too fast.
He'll always reach for my hand
        and he'll definitely heal my past.

He'll know I need reassuring often,
whilst the broken edges of my heart soften.
So whilst I love too much, too hard, too fast *for you.*
He'll be at my door, because he missed the view.
He won't leave me waiting
    because *he loves just the way I do.*

i will love you for evermore

FOR REAL

You remind me of the sun,
because you felt like all the best parts
                      were still to be done.
I didn't want to miss a moment with you,
because I knew at the end an infinity would still not do.

But as I sit alone now
    with just your memory for company,
I want to feel sad and *I know I have every right to be,*
but I don't feel that, instead I feel proud,
that you are choosing life
      and for that I want to cheer you on from the crowd.

I see that you are choosing laughter
    but I hope when you can,
in-between the healing, that *you finally see yourself*
                as the whole man,
who deserves to be loved completely,
and piece by piece you rebuild and *finally see.*

You remind me of a warm ocean breeze,
and every moment you looked at me
                  I wanted time to freeze.
Because I wanted forever with you.
I knew at the end an infinity would still not do.

But, we had to say goodbye,
because really for us staying was the biggest lie.
You have to walk this part without me.
Self sacrifice was the greatest gift I could see.

And maybe that's how *we know it's love for real,*
because saying goodbye,
        set us on this path to heal.

Amiee Laura Knubley

i will love you for evermore

Amiee Laura Knubley

i will love you for evermore

Dear you,

Loving you is my greatest blessing. How lucky am I to know someone who is filled with such light, such fire and such passion. I don't know if I ever say the words enough or if I ever show you in the right ways but I hope you know.

For when the sun shines I pray it is shining on you because I only ever want you to feel the warmth. Before the flowers bloom, know that I watered them for you so every day you would see a beauty as pure as yours. But when you fall, I promise I will carry you because you are no burden - you can set it down on me, always.

I hope that in between my arms you find your place, and with each embarce you know that I was never anyone elses. Not for a moment. Not for a breath. I waited my entire life for you and you my love are worth every bit.

So, if I haven't said it enough, I am sorry, but I thought you knew. If I haven't showed you enough, then let this letter be the start and what I will do. For I want you to feel my love always. Never a question.

Through the winters and the summers I will love you. In the madness and the chaos we will stand, for calmer waters will come, that I will make sure.

Loving you, is my greatest blessing.

Always,
Me.

- loving you

i will love you for evermore

What if this is it?
The moment when all the pieces fit.
The world could shatter,
but our story is the *only thing* that can matter.

When you say my name my skin is alive.
A fire within I'm never sure I'll survive.
I want to know *who you are,*
and every moment that has got you this far.

Can we find tomorrow, again?
Taking on the world in one lane.
Because when you've got me to love you,
I promise you there is nothing that you can't do.

I belong with you and you belong with me.
Promise me that this was always meant to be.

      - strangers

Amiee Laura Knubley

CHAPTER TWO

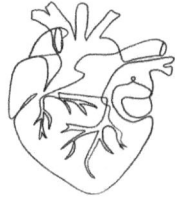

heartbreak
-

The collection of poems and letters that make up this chapter explore the depths of heartbreak from loss, grief and separation to the disappointment of unmet potential. Maybe to give you the words to describe the anger that rages through you or the sadness and despair that you are sat in now, or have already survived and are just looking to understand. There is no one size fits all for heartbreak but it is gritty and it is raw and shame stops us from communicating that. This collection is designed to show you that it is normal to feel whatever it is you feel, be that angry and hurt, sad, or lonely. It is ok to feel desperate and hopeless and in fact these feelings are necessary to grow as a human. It is what we *choose to do* with these feelings that sets us apart.

Poems like *'liar', 'black and white', 'your voice'* and *'victimless'* give rise to traumatic and toxic events that occur in society and the healing that individuals like you and I have to do from that. Losing yourself to something that took your light is fucking horrendous and writing about it and talking about it, for me, started the steps to reignite my light. Heartbreak, as we know too well, can come after the realisation that saying goodbye has to happen, when we don't want to, when we don't know how to; but by god for the good of reason, we have to. Poems like 'north star', 'lovers passed' and 'it was magic' open the mic to those moments of karmic connections, lessons for a reason and right person wrong time.

Writing 'the fight' came from a place of healing. Growing through the trauma of past love so we put our weapons down to feel the fear and fall anyway, trusting a new love and not treating what could be, like a new battle to win.

Whatever heartbreak you are feeling or have felt, I hope that you can stand tall knowing that no one situation can define you, unless you want it to. There is no right way to heal, but I hope reading this collection helps you take a step in the right direction where you can feel not so alone.

You are enough, you are important, and I promise you; you can do hard things.

I pray this collection takes you somewhere and gives you exactly what you need.

All my love,
Always, forever, for evermore,
Amiee

i will love you for evermore

i will love you for evermore

Dear you,

Isn't it time you got your voice back? I understand why you are in the place that you are in. It makes sense because I would be there too. But I can't wait for the day I hear you roar again. You were filled with such power because your tenderness gave you strength. People would listen to you and what you had to say mattered. I know it feels so long ago, but you will return. I promise you that.

Isn't it strange how something (*someone*) that used to make us feel whole, at the end can feel so much more powerful than us and you don't know how you got there. It wasn't a straight line of stepping stones that you can trace back to understand. It is like a ball of wool with stories woven that can never be un-spun. Tracing back the steps probably won't help now but I want you to know is, that it wasn't your fault. You did nothing wrong. Their power wasn't tender and their power wasn't a light but a dark that only grows by taking others by night. You know that though, you saw it happen to others.

I remember at the start when I heard you say the things you would never stand for and the words you would never allow. But overtime you were worn down so much that the big things became little things, and those little things became normal things, acceptable things; and your tenderness became weakness, and your voice became a whisper.

It is not your fault. I hope that if you know nothing else, this you can hear me say. It is not your fault that this happened and it is not your fault you are here.

i will love you for evermore

So now you see, isn't it time you got your voice back? You are enough and what you have to say matters. You are worthy and the things you care about are important. You have dreams and you can do hard things. I know it doesn't feel like it now, but in time it will. In time, you will stand, you will roar and you will be the voice for others that need to hear it too. After it all, know that you are loved.

Always,
The Universe

- your voice

i will love you for evermore

Dear you,
After all this time do you regret me?

- history

i will love you for evermore

So now you see, isn't it time you got your voice back? You are enough and what you have to say matters. You are worthy and the things you care about are important. You have dreams and you can do hard things. I know it doesn't feel like it now, but in time it will. In time, you will stand, you will roar and you will be the voice for others that need to hear it too. After it all, know that you are loved.

Always,
The Universe

> *- your voice*

i will love you for evermore

Dear you,
After all this time do you regret me?

- history

i will love you for evermore

Dear you,

I hope that after all that has passed now, you can see what you were meant to learn. Please don't get stuck in what you dreamed of with them. You were right, they were magic. Their eyes did make you lose yourself and you were not crazy because I promise you, they felt it too. Your connection was divine and the world did really disappear when you were together. It's just that this was only meant for a short time. Their presence in your life was only temporary. You see, some people are only meant to be temporary. No matter how right it feels, they aren't always meant to stay.

They came to wake you up, from the survival you were lost in. They came to give you warmth, to relight the fire that you need for tomorrow. You are love. You are light and the world needs that. You forgot that for a little bit there and they came to show you, remind you and help you be. *They did that didn't they?*

All those late night conversations so deep you could have both swam to the other side of the world. Their touch and their heart, every time you joined, like the one soul that you both are. They saw you, every piece, even the hidden that makes you, you. Didn't it feel like heaven on earth to be heard, seen and held like that? Yes? So, remember that? Not the loss you feel now.

The universe, god, your guardians or whatever it is you believe, has you. I promise you that what is meant for you never truly leaves. If they are meant to, they will return but it is not guaranteed so promise me that you will see now what you were meant to learn?

Always,
The Universe.

- it was magic

i will love you for evermore

GONE

Today *I miss you.*
That is not new but today, I've cried a lot too.
I saw a photo of you,
and I couldn't breathe because my heart knew,
that this single second would take me right back
    to the start.
Where again, I would have to forget and
    remove you from my heart.

Amiee Laura Knubley

i will love you for evermore

I didn't want to lose you.
But I'm not sure if you ever truly knew.
Knew what you wanted and if that was ever me.
You never said the words of *what we could be.*

I saw you caught up in your yesterday,
just waiting for it all to be ok.
I wanted to fix it all for you,
but this was *your journey,* the healing that you had to do.

- the saddest goodbye

i will love you for evermore

You made me feel alive and little less lost.
But it turns out we were just *could be lovers*
    with our wires crossed.
I dreamt of you often so I could see your face,
and feel your touch for a moment, forgetting the space.

Every so often I would actually hear your voice,
and after hours of laughing I forgot
        I never really had a choice.
Because you held the wheel
        always keeping me away so far,
and sometimes it felt like I was following you
    in a different car.

But loving you felt like breathing for me.
So of course staying was the only option
                that I could see.
Until my heart met my head,
and in the darkness my body wouldn't leave my bed.

"You're better than this", my head cried.
"Sit up sweet girl, at least you've tried.
"Stand proud, stand tall, fly like a bird,
and promise me next time you'll keep your word?"

        - your heart

i will love you for evermore

Amiee Laura Knubley

SILENCE

How is it when I wake, you fill my mind.
Yet you *forget* I exist.
Your skin is still under mine.
Your voice is an all consuming mist.
How is it that I let myself fall.
Always waiting for your call.

I need to find a way to break this high.
Come down from this, from you.
I just don't know how I'm meant to write *goodbye*,
to someone *who thinks just like I do.*
You've created an empty space between us now.
The silence is breaking through the how.

I'd never met my yellow until I met you.
But I'm left with the reality of the things you cannot do.
Just walk away, I can't make you see.
That you are the best thing that I could ever be.
Together the world would melt under our fire.
Everyday raising each other higher.

How is it that when I breathe you are my air.
Yet you even barely seem to care.
Your smile in every moment I leave behind.
How is it that I've let myself fall.
When I didn't mean for this at all.

DARE TO

You showed me,
the way that love wasn't meant to be.
I know love isn't silence, being alone or tears.
But you did just that to hold me in my fears.

I found you.
To share my light and to show you
         everything we could do.
I know love is brave, patient and kind,
But you ended up just hiding,
    in all the places that you could find.

For you, I wasn't enough.
Because loving me was apparently *so. damn. tough.*
I know that's not true, honest or fair.
It wasn't me at all, but simply because
        you. wouldn't. dare.

Dare to love bravely and free.
Dare to say it all, and shout your love for me.
Dare to just stay.
Dare to *not get in your own way.*

So, now I will show you,
a goodbye you will always regret having to do.
I'll always be your what if, a wonder and yes, maybe…
all because *you chose fear, over me.*

i will love for you evermore

LOVERS PASSED

I will always remember you like the summer sky.
Because *I* never wanted to say goodbye.
I've been waiting all my life for a love you cannot give.
So I walked away to find the love that I want to live.
And even though, to me you are perfection.
I need a love that won't feel like a daily rejection.

I will always remember you like the oceans blue,
because to me you felt like home, *but the moments
                            were too few.*
I can't wait to be held by someone who sees my light,
and for a life with me, well he's ready to fight.
Because he knows my love feels like honey,
and in-between the magic, life will always be
                       a little funny.

Even when I've met *him*, know that
                I will always remember you.
As someone who I hated passing by and who I loved
   through and *through*.
Because your soul was a mirror of mine,
and I *was* drawn to the way your light chose to shine.
So I will always remember *you*,
   like my favourite summer sky.
And when you miss me,
   remember that *I* never wanted to say goodbye.

Amiee Laura Knubley

LIAR

What is it that you stand for?
Because from here I think I misread you
    right to your core.
I thought you were honest and kind.
But in your silence *lies* are all I can find.

I drew you as a green wren.
As the promise of spring poured from my pen.
But each line of your feather was drawn with lies.
Because that's all you gave me between each of my
                                          cries.
I look at it now and I've never seen anything uglier.
And the story of us,
        well I can't think of anything funnier.

What is it that you stand for?
Because all I know is that I misread you
    right to your core.
I know that *I am honest and kind.*
And in my silence, regret is all you will find.

Amiee Laura Knubley

i will love you for evermore

NORTH STAR

I don't want to give up on you,
but I know that I have to.
I'm not the same after knowing you.
I've got all this strength but no idea what I should do.
I have to say goodbye,
but *it feels like stars giving up the sky.*

i will love you for evermore

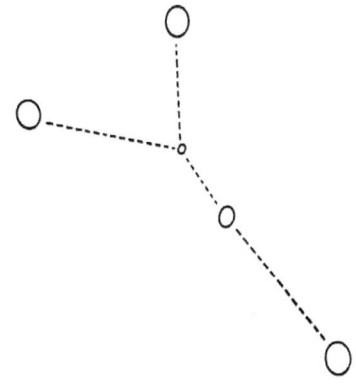

Amiee Laura Knubley

BEFORE YOU

When I say I miss you,
know that I mean it like its the only words that are true.
But forgive me if I stumble and fall,
when I try to say it all.
I know my words well
but saying this, *it feels like a clumbsy story to tell.*

No words could ever really express it.
A shot so far I could never really hit.
When you say goodbye
    I suddenly feel like I can't breathe.
I wake wondering how you are so *familiar* to me,
when last year I didn't even know that you could be.

i will love you for evermore

i will love you for evermore

i will love you for evermore

LETS NOT SAY GOODBYE

Goodbye is the hardest word to say.
One word, two syllables, but it takes my breath away.
So, let's not say goodbye.
I'll just say thank you for your love
         because it means I can now fly.

Please don't feel guilty or let the sadness stay too long.
Those are not the words I want to hear
    in *your* life song.
You couldn't have done anymore for me.
Time had its way just as it was meant to be.
I felt your heart and I know that you would have come.
I heard your prayers because each word
         had a magical hum.

I wasn't alone and I wasn't scared.
But saying goodbye was the hardest part, knowing just how much everyone cared.
    I just wish I had more time as me.
For one last time I could sing and dance
         to my favourite melody.

I promise that I will visit you often,
and I hope that when you feel me near your fear
         will soften,
because sweet girl, you are an inspiring woman now,
and I'm proud of you doing it all,
    with *absolutely* no idea how.

Goodbye is the hardest word to say.
So, let's not say goodbye *today.*

Amiee Laura Knubley

i will love you for evermore

I WILL MISS YOU

I will miss you.
Before I close my eyes each night,
I'll try not to call, taking everything I have to fight.

I will miss you.
When I'm sitting at the ocean thinking of tomorrow,
I'm reminded of all the seeds that we had left to sow.

I will miss you.
When I'm choosing songs to play,
and all I want is to hear the funny joke that you'd say.

I will miss you.
Every-time I pick up my phone to see,
because it is your name that I want it to be.

I will miss you.
Even when I've met someone new,
because our souls knew that *we were not yet through*.

I will miss you.
In every moment in between these.
Even though you left too soon and you walked away
with such ease.

i will love you for evermore

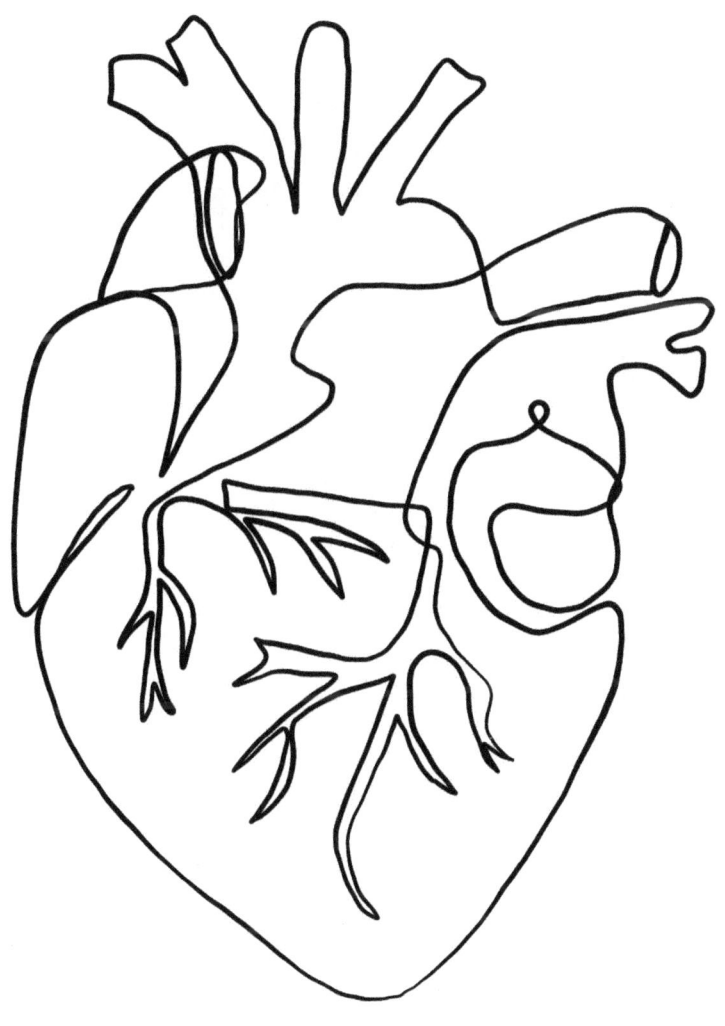

i will love you for evermore

Amiee Laura Knubley

i will love you for evermore

THANK MY YOU OLD FRIEND

I am not often speechless because I have never had a problem with words. They come to me in a flourish, like I imagine a song does for our beautiful mocking birds. *But with this choice, I don't know what to say.* My mind feels cloudy and the tears so easily find their way.

They said it is time and of course that's expected - your body is miraculously old. But you see, on me, your heart still has its *hold*. How am I meant to say goodbye, *my dear old friend.* I don't think after this one, my heart will be able to fully mend.

It will be left a little misshapen but of course more full after knowing you, and after tomorrow, *our memories will have to do.*

Love is like a wildfire and yours burns so bright. You, my old friend shared this with me, your light. Saying thank you doesn't feel like its enough, Because you never left my side even when the days got really tough.

I don't know how to tell the others about tomorrow.
Maybe for a moment, you could give me your courage, just to borrow? This is the hardest goodbye we will all do. But our lives are better, *simply for knowing you.*

I know your eyes are tired, and your paws even more so. I'm not surprised because you've been the most loyal shadow. Thank you for loving us in every moment, of every day, but you can close your eyes now, I promise I'll be here every step of the way.

Just promise me you will come visit again real soon.
We will look out for you, in every rainbow, butterfly and star - and of course on the *brightest moon.* Thank you my old friend, *I will love you always, and I'll see you again, when I meet my end.*

Amiee Laura Knubley

VICTIMLESS

My problem was I didn't know when to let go.
Even when I was screaming
    "why must you hurt me so".
I told myself I couldn't give up or walk away.
I'd invested too much and I knew what they'd say.

"She said forever".
They wouldn't question him whatsoever.

"I knew she would break his heart".
Protecting him like he never played his part.

Years went by and piece by piece he broke me.
And still I never found my feet to be the bravest
    they could be.
With them leading the way, I never would leave him,
because when I said forever,
    I didn't mean a hundred meter swim.

Looking back now, I think the worst part,
was not that he left looking like some fine art.
Because I knew he would lie in the stories he told,
but it was that *I lost my courage*,
    that after it all,
        I couldn't be bold.

i will love you for evermore

Dear you,

After all this time do you regret me? This question plays on my mind. The years that went by, the pain and the loss. I mean how could you not? I couldn't give you what I promised. You couldn't keep yours, but I'd like to know what crosses your mind, even after all this time.

I had the learn to put one foot in front of the other. After you left.

I don't think you realise the chaos you created. You didn't look back. *Not once.* But you threw those daggers every chance you could get. The person you once loved, did I ever exist to you? Sometimes I think about the what if. What if I had left all those years ago?

Our love wasn't true and could never see us through. How could it? But you helped me survive. When my world crashed it was only you. For that I'm grateful.

Forever grateful.

You helped me survive.
When the room felt dark, you made it lighter.
When I lost my words, you spoke.
When I couldn't walk, you carried me.

You're the reason I still exist and for that reason *I thank you*. It was you, when the world began to fall. I still don't understand how you chose this at all. I don't think I will ever understand but I'd like know what crosses your mind, even after all this time?

Never again,
Me.

- *never again*

LIGHT

Burn bright we need your light.
Burn bright love of the night.
Don't tell me you are…
Speechless.
Dreamless.
Hopeless.

See, you need not *my* forgiveness.

What happened to you?
Love of the night.

What happened to you?
Blinded in full sight.

What happened to you?
Hidden by your light.

Can it not always be?
Well, that I understand.

But don't tell me you are still…
Speechless.
Dreamless.
Hopeless.

Darling, you need not *my forgiveness.*

It is with you.
It was only ever on you.

i will love you for evermore

BLACK AND WHITE

It was black and white,
that with every breath you were ready to fight.
I had done no wrong,
yet you looked at me like I didn't belong.
Your eyes burned with fire,
and when you looked at me I knew
    I would be called the liar.

As quiet as a mouse,
I tried to move around our house.
Because the moment you saw me,
I didn't know *what would be.*
How did years come to this?
Along the way *what signs did I miss?*

Amiee Laura Knubley

i will love you for evermore

GOODBYE

No, you don't get to stand there after you just disappeared.
You left and brought up everything my heart feared.
How dare you tear down my wall,
and then walk away like nothing happened at all.

"You were made for me" you lied.
"You're amazing" you cried.
"How are you so strong?".
"You're inspiring", smiling, like I could do no wrong.

Well, I fell for it all.
Answering *every bloody* call.
You bet I feel stupid.
I believed every word like some gullible kid.

I started to think in dreams.
Trusting that everything was as honest as it seemed.
Well I don't trust twice you see.
So, walk away now and just let me be.

i will love you for evermore

Baby, I see your camouflage now I do.
I'm curious how did you pick the perfect colour
so I would believe you?

You said close your eyes, fall into me.
But when I fell, an empty space was all I could see.

I hope I made you feel good,
but I only wish now that *I understood.*

- lies

Amiee Laura Knubley

i will love you for evermore

SORRY

You will never hear the words 'I'm sorry'.
But you don't need them you see?
You have the power because you can let go,
without ever needing him to know.

You don't need an apology,
for every time he owed you the speech of, *'I'm sorry'*.
Because you'll be standing there forever,
listening to him justify each time he went, *hell* for *leather*.

There is nothing he can say to take back each time.
And it won't help if others know each and every crime.
You already have peace and you already know.
That is enough to end this crazy shit show.

i will love you for evermore

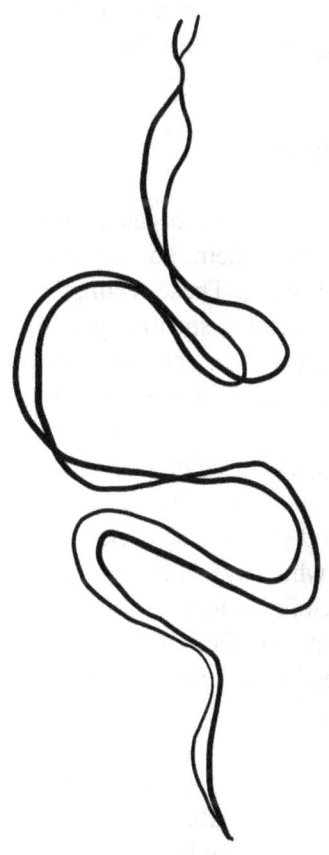

i will love you for evermore

Dear you,

I say this with love and by no means to minish the hurt you feel and how hard this person leaving you is. A marriage ending is somewhat catastrophic, but I say this as someone who has come out the other side. This will not and can not be the end of you. A person who has hurt you, betrayed you and left you will not be the reason you stop living. You will not give them power to stop you from smiling, laughing, falling in love, seeing light in your day.

You cannot let them.

So feel what you need, because you have to feel these things to process them, so they can leave your body, but do not sit there. These feelings will take over you, mentally, physically, spiritually, and you have already spend too long with it. I can see it in your eyes, the way you hold yourself, recoil from people.

It took me years. Goddam years and I do not want that for you. You were magnificent before them, pure magic with them and you will be even more after them. There are people who have survived traumatic life events, physical abuse, loss, torture and they have, not all I will give you that, but the majority have survived, grown and blossomed into the next chapter of their life, so that means you will too.

You see, it is a choice, how we choose to move forward, how we choose to talk to ourselves, the healing we choose to do, each step is a choice. So I am begging you to just start. I promise on the other side you will see why I pushed you.

Always,
Me.

- the separation

Amiee Laura Knubley

i will love you for evermore

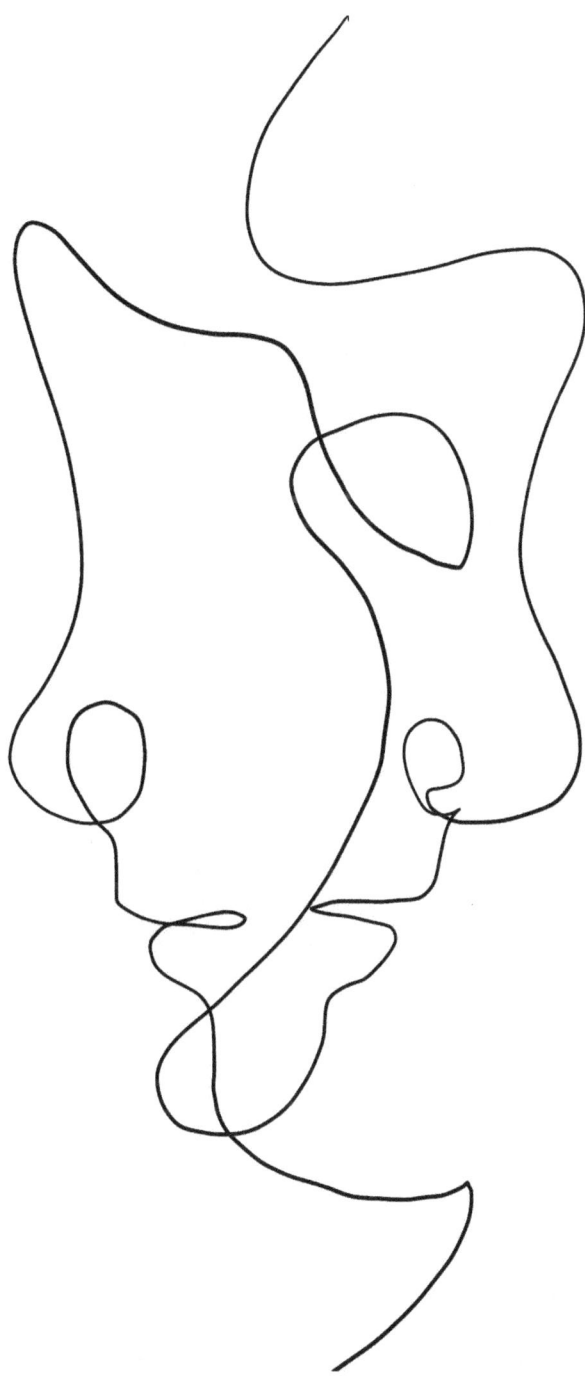

Amiee Laura Knubley

CHAPTER THREE

motherhood

-

This collection of poems and letters are contradictory in a way. They speak of the purest form of love one human can have for another. A love you would give your life for as a mother. A love that fills you with immense pride, hope and joy but also one that fills you with fear; and can destroy your peace in an instant. They speak to a role that mothers have in life, where you never truly understand both sides, until the doing begins.

Not every mothers journey to motherhood is created equal and poems like *'miscarriage'*, *'infertility'* and *'infertile promise'* give you the words for exactly that. For they are mothers. They speak to a time where an abandonment of hope is inconceivable, for it is the only reason you wake up in the morning. A desperate, soul crushing hope that keeps you moving, searching for a light in a pitch black room. That is the room pure warriors are made, and these women will never give up on anything, ever again, *but* without a second thought they will walk away from anything that costs them their peace. They have learned themselves to their inner most being.

Poems like *'my son'*, *'I promise'* and *'dear heart'* encompass the true weight of expectations. For are you truly a mother if you have not disappointed people you do not know, with words unsaid, because of things you ought to be feeling, doing and saying, to live up to the expectations set on you; before you were even born?

Becoming a mother was everything, but also nothing like I expected it to be. Daily I am filled with an unexplainable love that gives me life, but it is wrapped so very nicely in fear, and doubt and with a bow of exhaustion. Being a mother has taught me more about myself than I ever thought I needed to learn and it has also pushed me to extremes within myself, that I am grateful I now know exist.

Motherhood is spectacular, and whilst we may not all want to or can become mothers, we all have a mother. There is a lot to be learned about love from that perspective. Our ancestors are filled with love in a form that has to be talked about, to be passed down through generations. A line of women, who became mothers and stood up in the world with no idea how, but with love they did the best they could, with the tools they had at the time. Some failed and created immense pain but most took each step with love. The line may not be filled with perfect mothers, ambitious or inspirational women but each line of mothers are filled with truth, history and meaning. For without them we wouldn't even exist.

I pray this collection takes you somewhere and gives you exactly what you need.

All my love,
Always, forever, for evermore,
Amiee

i will love you for evermore

Amiee Laura Knubley

MOTHER ENOUGH

They make me laugh a little louder.
And of their courage I couldn't be prouder.
They make me better than yesterday,
giving me the space to find my way.

I'm living the dream I used to pray for.
So when they reach for me I will give,
    even when there is nothing left to pour.
For this love is not given with conditions, you see.
because my child stands with all the best parts of me.
They will grow and the will learn *who they are,*
and I know it is *my love* which will carry them so far.

So when *I am tired* and I want to give up on this,
I will allow my self to rest because being their mother
    isnt something I want *to miss.*

When *I am angry* and when I can't think,
and all this pressure is bringing me to the brink.
    ...I will sit and breathe,
knowing *really* I don't ever want to leave.

When *I am lonley* and think about my life before,
I will allow myself to cry
    and then knock on my best friends door,
because I am not alone in this journey,
and its ok to disagree *that a mother is all I can be.*

For I am brave and I am strong,
and being a mother is only *part of my song.*
But I will sing that part loud,
and on the days where simply I cannot stand
    I will remember loving my child is enough,
and that makes me so very proud.

Amiee Laura Knubley

i will love you for evermore

I PROMISE

I am trying so hard to give you the love that I needed then. I don't want you to think of your mother and remember rejection
>*again and again.*

So I hope with me you know you'll always have a home. Your heart is held and you will never ever have to roam.

You will feel my presence wherever you go.
Even in the little voice you've developed so you don't ever, *not know,* how to be kind *now* because that's all you knew, how to be brave as you step because you learned that from me too.

You won't ever not know. Because I held your hand when it mattered, *when you couldn't go.* You never felt alone or afraid of what was to be, because you had together where you always had me. I painted in colour and gave each brush to you, so you learned who you were and want you wanted to do.

Each night I caught the moon, so she would shine on you and not leave a moment too soon. I became the sun, the rain, and the stars in the sky. I held space *for what you needed* so you felt safe to finally fly.

I hope at the end you'll hold my hand, and we'll tell our epic stories because *without me*
>*they are your marching band.*

A guide for you, forever, because when I am gone, *they will be your tether.* To the first love you knew.
The one who showed you magic, who always believed
>in you.

I hope at the end you'll know how love creates its hum, because everyday you met her, in me, *your mum.*

Amiee Laura Knubley

i will love you for evermore

MY SON

Each week you get to take a part of me,
and for a few days I exist *aimlessly*.
I know we didn't plan to live like this,
but some kindness wouldn't go a miss.

He loves you, more than you would ever know,
and I just have to smile like I chose this show.
You see sometimes this does feel like a dance,
where I'm just spinning, and never given a chance.
A chance to be me, even though *it was you that set us free*.

As you drive away with my heart in the car,
I hope and pray that *at least for him* love is the lowest bar.
Sharing my child wasn't something I thought I would do.
This give and take for him, *with you*.

I hope he knows that he is loved,
and for years he was all I had dreamed of.

I'd give my sweet boy everything,
but one home and a *'normal family'* isn't what we can bring.
Instead we will stand separately.
Two pillars protecting him so carefully.

For it is in kindness he will grow,
not this ego driven, one man show.
So the next time you speak to me,
please choose your words so very carefully.
For our boy is watching.
He is carefully *listening*,
and it is in these moments that he will see
the type of man, *he will try to be.*

Amiee Laura Knubley

i will love you for evermore

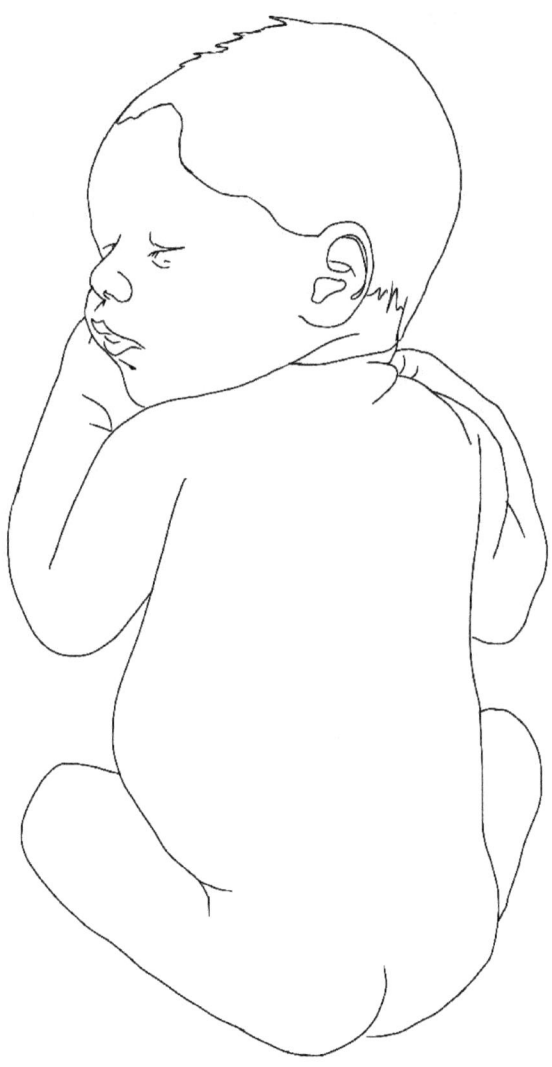

Amiee Laura Knubley

HER

You stand here now because of her sacrifices before.
She fought, she loved and *she always gave a little bit
more.*

So think of her in everything you do.
Because without her strength, well,
you wouldn't be you.

i will love you for evermore

i will love you for evermore

DEAR HEART

You are everything I dreamed you would be.
You might have my eyes but that knowing,
    that is not from me.
You hold the world in your hands already,
and every answer is in your mind *holding you steady.*

You are all the best parts of me.
You feel in colour and you dream
    of *everything* that could be.
You love with no fear,
and that my darling *will always keep the magic near.*

You speak so clearly and with such conviction,
but your tender heart is what holds their attention.
I am so proud of you for everything that you are.
For every win, but especially each time you
    actually missed the bar,
because trying matters more,
than any win you that you have received before.

Dear heart know this,
these are the words that you cannot miss…
Trust yourself and remember who you are.
I am your mother and I was a fighter but when I feel far,
know that you've got my courage and fight,
because I poured my love into you so
    you would be the brightest light.

Oh sweet boy, I will love you forever and always.
My life with you, *those were my very best days.*

Amiee Laura Knubley

i will love you for evermore

MY WISH FOR YOU

I wish I could see the point on the horizon,
so I could you prepare you for the moment
    before its gone.
The point when all your dreams come true,
because that is all I wish for you.

Your life will be so big and bold,
and filled with so much joy and love to hold.
I know you will be brave and stand up after each fall,
because you my child, will be the strongest of all.

Learning comes from trying and that is something
    I wish I was taught.
I could only ever win and a failure would never
        be caught.
But to look at the loss is important for growing.
You have to sit with it before you can keep going.

Your life will have pain and sorrows.
I wish I could take it from all of your tomorrows.
But I can't and I shouldn't,
because if I did, you wouldn't see the light,
    you just wouldn't.

So, my job you see now,
is to teach you the how.
To dance when the sun shines on you,
and that riding out the storm is what you will do.

I can't wait to see what you will be.
But know that really, *in reality,*
I will love you no matter what you do,
and *I will give anything*
    to make life abundant and light, for you.

Amiee Laura Knubley

i will love you for evermore

LA LUNE

You know that I love the moon,
just as much as I hate all the moments gone too soon.
I cry at sunsets, butterflies and rainbows,
because they are a reminder that wherever we go, *love flows*.

I make wishes on eyelashes, on dandelion fairies and on each
    shooting star.
Always hoping that I haven't gone too far.
For a while I dreamed,
    that my reality wasn't what it seemed.

You see the dark came for a while.
I lost my heart, all my hope, my beautiful smile.
It took a long time to find me.
I searched in all the corners and the dark holes that I could see.

But I only found the empty.
The silence and the reminder of what I couldn't be.
Until one day, the sun fell on my face.
The warm light of a forgiving grace.

I don't know how and I don't know why.
But it was then that the darkness faded from the sky.
Each day was easier than the last.
The dark no longer hanging like my mast.

It is now that I can proudly say,
    that even with the darkness of yesterday,
my world is beautiful, abundant and bright.
Each moment I take a step and *I choose the light.*

I'm so glad that I am alive,
I'm so proud that I survived.
So every night I'll look for the moon,
    and wish that this moment won't pass me by too soon.

Amiee Laura Knubley

i will love you for evermore

Nocturnal was she,
a wanderer, a traveler was what she desired to be.
On a plight to no where,
   or maybe everywhere,
whispered, she.

Nocturnal was he,
a believer, a dreamer, was what he hoped to be.
On a plight to nowhere,
   and maybe everywhere.
cried, he.

For you.
   Because there was nothing else that they could do.

        - miscarriage

Amiee Laura Knubley

i will love you for evermore

Oh, how much is left to burn?
What could possibly be left to learn.
Chasing laps around the sun.
I'm not sure in a past life what I could have done.
    But please forgive me is what I hear in my cries,
because we have seen the waters rise.

And whilst the mountains and sky fall,
I worry this will be nothing at all.
We can't rush this moment even though
                we've cried every day.
    You will find us, I don't care what they say.
No one knows how long, but *regardless*,
    we will wait for you.

Until the end of time, this fight is all I will do.
My sweet child, we will wait for you.
    Until the end of time, this fight is what I will do.

        - infertility

i will love you for evermore

I know your love is the reason why,
that my soul is breathing, directed at the sky.
But maybe our lives our destined for beyond the
    stars,
        and in this world,
                our story,
  might not actually be ours.

Light up the way.
Take my ocean of tears and say,
come like grace again *for* I am breaking.
My feet, my knees, are shaking.

Even when strength is lost I will stand for you.
I will survive the breaking, *even if its the last thing I will do.*
    I will stand for you.
For it is all I know how to do.

          - grief

April 4th

Dear my child,

I need to write to you today. For the first time I truly feel like giving up on you. You feel so far away and it feels like the existence of you will only ever be in my dreams. I need to feel close to you, thinking one day you might read this. This thought is all that is keeping me going. I'm tired my love. My throat hurts from holding back my tears. I'm losing myself and I'm angry that we are still here, doing this.

I've been thinking about your name. It helps me believe that one day you will be real. I've been looking at names that embody who I dream you to be. You will be someone who survives. Someone who is born from this shit storm is going to be epitome of strength and pure love. My love you are going to be so very strong with a fight that will mean you can truly survive anything. You will have such grace because you existence will be the answer to my prayers. You will be so determined but driven by love, by your heart because you exist because of my unwavering love for you. You, no doubt will have so may other qualities, but these are what I imagine create you.

Gosh, thinking of who you might be makes my heart ache. I want to know you more than anything in the world. I question whether maybe I love too much and the universe just wants me to back off. I love so intensely. That is something that makes me who I am though and I love hard. I love very openly and I wear my heart on my sleeve. I hope you do that too.

I think there is a great courage and bravery in loving so openly and as often as we can. Vulnerability is hard but when you can master it, I think you feel a sense of peace. A relief. We are built for love after all.

i will love you for evermore

I am afraid that I might be stuck in this place forever. This inbetween, before you. I know that I will still have a life filled with love and joy, but I will also have this emptiness that I know will never leave. If I don't get the tomorrow with you. If we don't ever get to meet, I am not sure what will be left of me, because youhave taken most of my heart already. How could you not?

If this cycle works you will be born in December. This will make you an element of fire. You will be generous and funny. You will be curious and your open mind will be why you search for meaning in everything. You will be optimistic and so very driven. You will travel and value freedom. I am a water element. This means that I am driven by my emotions. I feel so very intensly. But, I am brave, passionate and stubborn. I am kind but I am fierce.

I cannot wait to teach you everything that I have learned about life, but for now I will wait.

All my love,
Your mum.

i will love you for evermore

In what order do I remember you?
Before I lost you, or will after have to do?

What will hurt my heart less?
the dream of what was or this grief ridden mess.

I think I'll remember the before.
Isn't that what a story tellers mind is for?

This way, to see you I just have to *close my eyes,*
and your face is there with a sweet beauty
                                       that matches the skies.
We're walking now in this memory of mine.
Your little feet are skipping as we travel along
                                       the coastline.
As you grow it becomes our place, the oceans blue…

   Ah, a silly little memory that never got to come true.

                  - hope

i will love you for evermore

Amiee Laura Knubley

i will love you for evermore

i will love you for evermore

Every night I look for you out amongst
the stars in the sky,
and in the quiet of that moment I always whisper
goodnight,
as my never ending goodbye.
For a moment I feel your light, like the magic will do,
but the heartbreak, grief and longing always breaks
through.

- *loss*

i will love you for evermore

Don't lean on me.
Don't count on what I can be.
I'm searching for forever.
I'm searching for you, even if the answer is never.
You see I just can't make the flowers grow.
No matter how many seeds I sow.

Let me give you my wish and you can hold it tight.
Maybe together we will be an even brighter light.
Whilst I search for forever.
Whilst I search for you in the never.
Maybe you can make the flowers grow.
With the seeds that I *used* to sow.

In the valleys of time, the promise I made, will stay.
But just in case we never meet
    and I never get the chance to say,
know that I will *not* let go.
until I can make the flowers grow.

When my shadow turns into a ghost,
I know that time will be what I've abused the most.
I'm searching for forever.
I'm searching for you, in the promise of never.

I watch the smiles as I fall.
I don't know why they think I can't have it all.
How dare they ask me
    why can't I make the flowers grow.
But I cannot and will not let the humiliation show.

Because you my child, *will be,*
and you will be so proud I didn't give up on you,
        a mere possibility.

  - *infertile promise*

i will love you for evermore

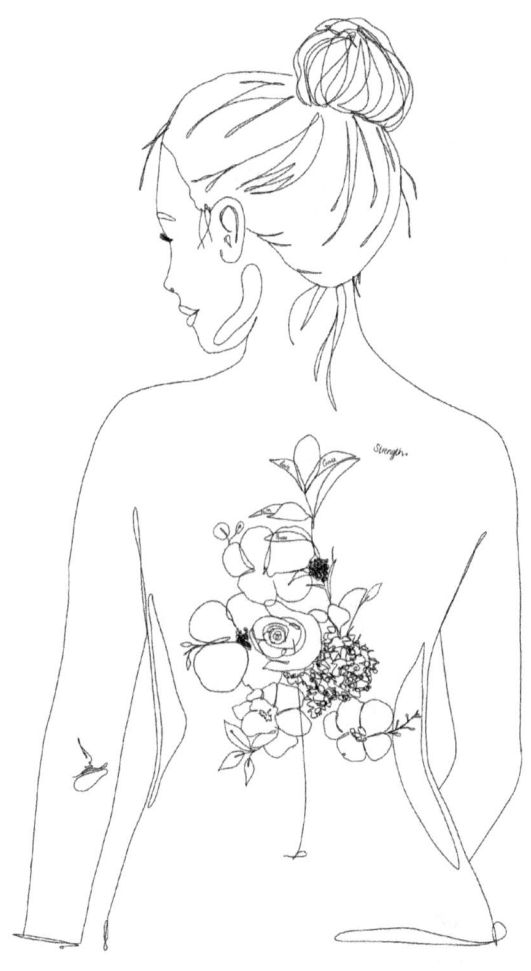

Amiee Laura Knubley

GREEN

Green is your colour.
The colour of life.
The earth, the body and mind.
The secrets of the ocean.
Green, is the colour of you.

Mine?
Mine, you can almost see.
Yellow like the sun, dry like the heat.
Just like the sand under your feet.
I say, not yet paradise,
always a second away.

Yellow?
Yellow is the colour of me.
Green is your colour.
Like the water in the falls.
Like the salt in the sea.
Honey to a bee.
The ocean deep.
Green is the colour of you.

My body and mind?
Yellow like a light but with water in my lungs.
Fire in my skin,
undone within.
Yellow, is the colour of me.

I can't do what I am meant to do.
I can't do what you can do.
Don't drown with me my love.

Green is the colour of life.

Green is the colour of *you*.

Amiee Laura Knubley

i will love you for evermore

Amiee Laura Knubley

i will love you evermore

June 19th

Dear my little Luna,

Today the universe has shown me how cruel and unfair life can be, but I can't let that take over. It took 548 days of treatment so that the universe would let you exist, let you grow with me, your mum. My darling when I saw those two lines they were so strong; there was no mistaking that you were here. I felt a joy so strong it matched your existence. My heart felt like it was whole again.

I cried. I cried at the prospect of meeting you, at all of the possibilities of who you would become. Of who I was now, your mother and I would become, your best friend. I cried. Your dad? He laughed. He smiled. He smiled at the thought of making you smile, of holding you and being your safe place. He smiled at the thought of his arms feeling like home. His smile made me smile and so our journey began.

Each test and each scan showed us that you were still here fighting with us and my darling we loved you from the moment we knew you were here. We fought for you. Please know that. We only had you with us for a short time but my darling my love, you were our light, our sun, our moon. You rebuilt my heart and reminded me of a love that I had forgotten could ever exist for me, for us. You were the light in the darkness that has been infertility. I dreamt of your hair blowing in the breeze as we sat by the sea. I dreamt of your eyes as big and bright as the ocean that I have sat at and prayed at, for you. You gave me and your dad a chance to dream of endless possibilities with you.

God decided that you were too precious for this world so we have lost you for now. But only for a little while my darling.

Amiee Laura Knubley

i will love you evermore

We will see you again. Every-time we look up at the moon, we will see you, feel you. A light so bright, you will always be. Thank you for being with us for this time my darling. Your life gave us so much hope and gave us so much love.

Our beautiful little Luna, forever we will think of you.

Always, to infinity,
Your mum.

PHEONIX

Like a light in the night,
you will always be.

Just as the flowers bloom and the sun rises,
you will always be.

A pebble in the water,
a friend and a daughter;
you will always be.

A phoenix in flight,
with the sea in its sight,
you will always, be.

i will love you evermore

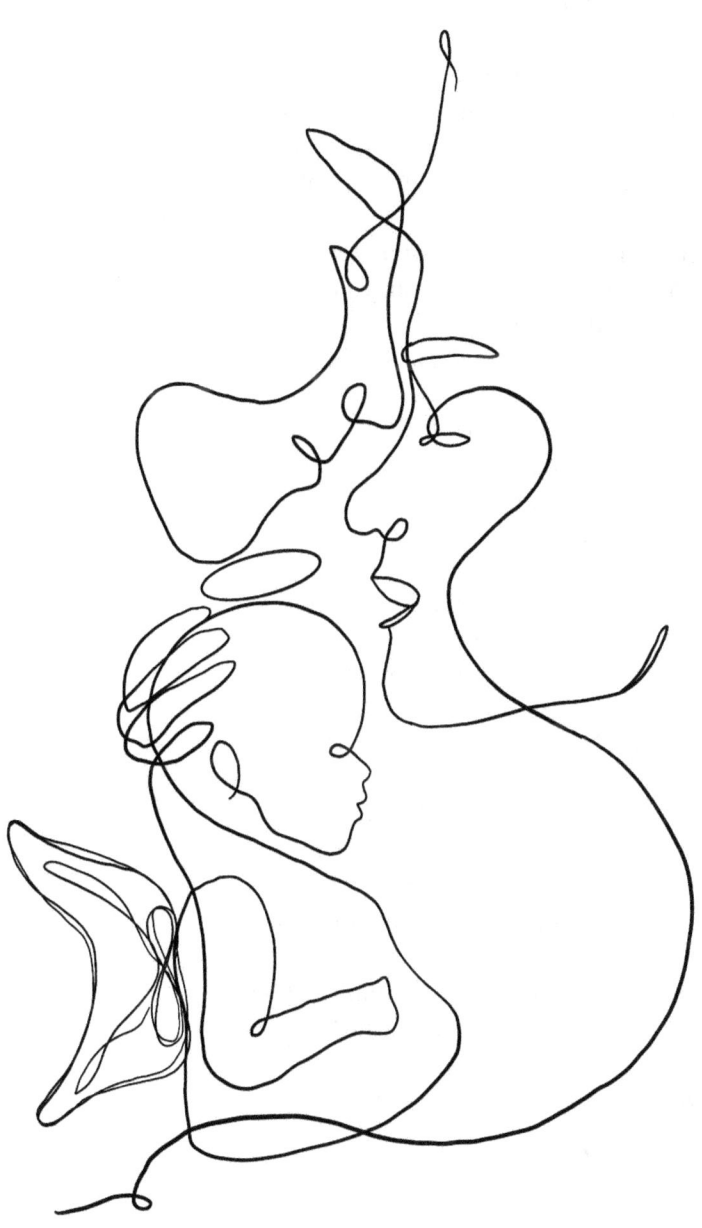

Amiee Laura Knubley

i will love you for evermore

FOR LUNA

How does it feel to be on the other side.
Of the heartbreak, the loss and all those tears you cried.
When your little boy hugs you tight,
you feel his strength and your fight.

He is here now because you never gave up hope.
That is your greatest power, *your ability* to cope.
Your resilience got you so far,
but really it was *hope* that set the bar.

You've grown around your grief but I still see it,
the hole in your heart that doesn't quite fit.
When your alone it has this hammering sound,
But you've learned to keep it quiet in the background.

You knew she was gone when you heard the words,
    "there is no heartbeat",
Four words that simply tripped you off your feet.
It was then you could have given up completely,
because losing a child changes you *inexplicably*.

And for a while you sat in sadness.
You believed it was your fault, all this mess.
Now you walk differently.
The air around you holds on more intently.

Because despite it all, it is your ability to think in dreams,
to know the dark isn't always what it seems.
This is what inspires me now,
because to stand up after that, I cannot even fathom how.

i will love you for evermore

So, how does it feel that you not only survived,
you've inspired, you've loved, you've thrived.
I am proud of you.
Because giving up was the easy thing to do.

How does it feel *to be on the other side.*
Your son is here now because you swam *through* that riptide.
That is your greatest power, your ability to cope.
Your resilience got you so far, but really it was *hope.*

Amiee Laura Knubley

i will love you for evermore

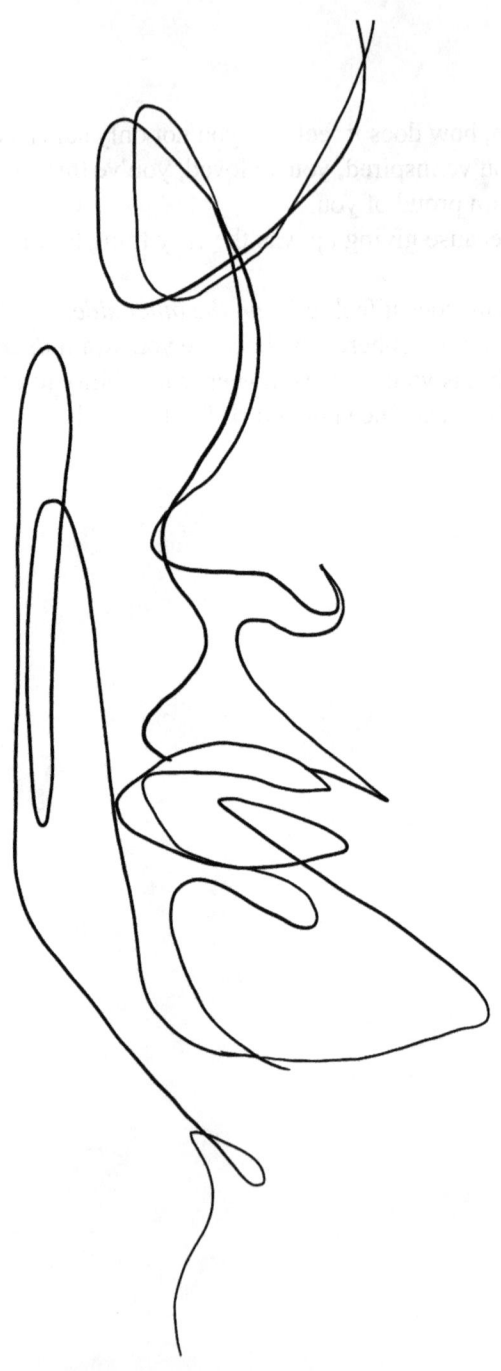

i will love you for evermore

MOTHERHOOD

I know its scary when you think of everything you
don't know, and you are exhausted from not letting the
fear show.

But you are not alone.

No mother was given a rule book to call her own.
We all think *"what the fuck"*, and put every win down
to beginners luck.

In the night it seems worst. The isolation and the
feeling that you might actually burst, from the sadness
and the doubt, but also the love and never ending joy.
    It is confusing I know,
                  and maybe that is the biggest ploy.
So we don't give up and quit this job,
because *I know I wanted to* in-between each sob.

I'll say it again and I promise you this,
this worry will be shared with *pure bliss.*
You will find your way.
Just remember to say,
    'I am not alone'.
We have to feel it and we cannot be shown,
for that is how the best *mothers are grown.*

Amiee Laura Knubley

CHAPTER FOUR

SELF

The collection of poems and letters in this chapter explore the themes of who we see ourselves as, and what we stand for, or are willing to fall for, in the theme of love; as this book foretells. I don't think a lot of people achieve the level of self love that the experts seem to talk about, but a good place to start in my opinion is acceptance and maybe a little bit of gratitude for ourselves.

Our identities are often so wrapped up in comparison and in believing that we fall short of the person we admire or aspire. This meaning somehow that we are worth less. That is the thing about our mind, it is a great story teller. It is capable of creating this image of ourselves through shame and self doubt; and we are left believing it all as fact. It just isn't true. We are breaking our own hearts. Questioning our purpose, direction, talents and skills. Wouldn't it be a truly magical conversation to have with ourselves if we could praise ourselves for a job well done, admire the work we have created, even see ourselves as the magic we were made to be, or exactly as others see us.

It has been said that to have love in our lives we have to be a whole person, be able to love ourselves before we can love another, but I disagree. I think what is vital is to know who we are, what we stand for, our true core values and beliefs.

Are you driven by curiosity, knowledge and growth? Is family your defining value that you will die on a sword for? Do you find purpose in your career or is it in your faith where you find peace? I think, that these don't change overtime. Of course growth and change is essential and the epitome of being human but when we truly sit and listen to our inner most truest voice, what we stand for doesn't often change and healing involves coming back to that, coming back to our selves, returning when we seem to have forgotten who we are.

Poems like *'what now?'*, *'self belief'* and *'too far'* look to explore the feelings associated to the importance we place on our direction, our purpose and our choices. Why do we get so frustrated when we feel we have steered off track, when things aren't following our plan. Maybe, it's because we have taken a few too many steps away from what really aligns. The *'little things'* and *'anything less'* serve as a reminder that being yourself is all you have to be. That is enough. What you have to offer is important and you are worthy of love just as you are.

This collection explores the raw and gritty that our mind presents us with and I hope that *'war'*, *'you are everything'* and *'it's ok'* help you see that you are not alone with feeling stuck, helpless or not enough. I hope you can learn to sit with yourself and maybe start with one small thing that is truly amazing. From there you can build on that?

I pray this collection takes you somewhere and gives you exactly what you need.

All my love,
Always, forever, for evermore.
Amiee

i will love you for evermore

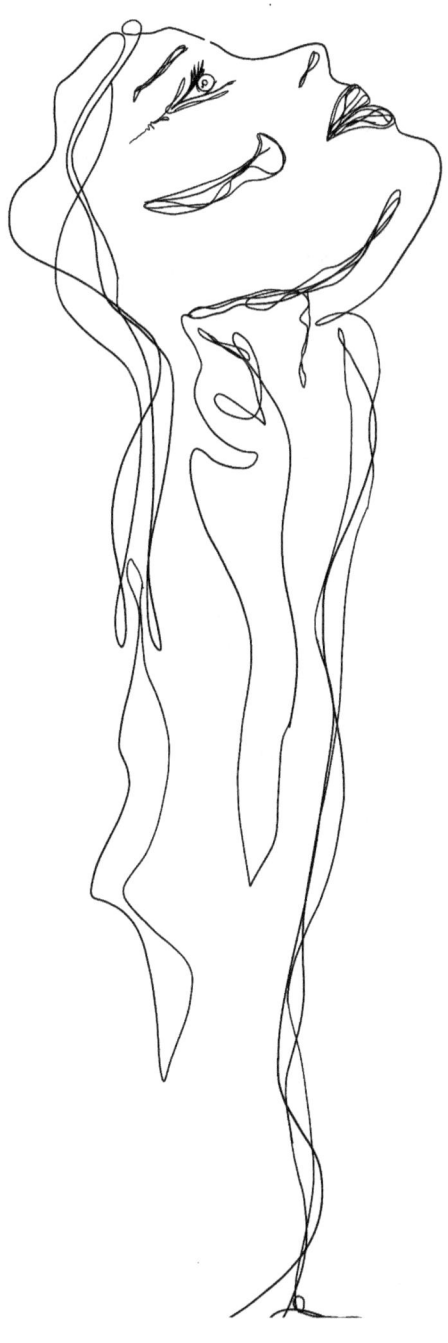

Amiee Laura Knubley

TOMORROW

I'm standing on the edge, the cusp of tomorrow.
A big beautiful beginning now that I have survived
                                  my low.
I can feel the magic, the light, just out of reach,
    just right there.
It is a new chapter and I know it is for us to share.

I feel this burning within, like the sun
    is hiding in my heart.
Ready to explode so tomorrow and I won't be apart.
I feel the edge of the cliff under my feet.
Just one more step and it is my next chapter that
                  I will meet.

I've never felt so ready to begin,
to open my arms and welcome it all in.
I'm ready to step and start the free fall.
I don't know what's coming, I know nothing at all.

What I do know about this feeling,
is that tomorrow is coming.
And I can't wait to meet it,
    to cry when all the pieces fit.

Amiee Laura Knubley

i will love you for evermore

PERFECTLY DESIGNED

You were made the same way as a flower in bloom.
So perfectly designed *but it's the worst you assume.*
You see the scars, the imperfections and the lies,
and in doing so you miss that the sun has left glimmers
                                      in your eyes.
Pieces of yellow and amber that radiate grace,
so that where ever you go, you leave hope in it's place.

You were made the same way as the feathers on a bird.
So perfectly designed even the angels have heard.
You see your pain as if it is written on your face.
But with every glance you don't see the that in fact
    kindness is your place.
Your words could heal the wounded at war.
To love, *that is what you exist on this earth for.*

You were made the same way that a snowflake
                                      should fall.
So perfectly designed with absolutely no question at all.
Where you see darkness,
            is in fact your never tiring fight.
Because you know you can't have the shadows
                        with out the suns light.
Your courage is immeasurable.
    So even in the bleakest winter storm,
I know you can open you eyes and remind everyone
                      that *soon a rainbow will form.*

Amiee Laura Knubley

i will love you for evermore

You already know what is to be.
   I just need to know that you are with me.
Eye to eye.
Hand in hand.
And not a single whisper of goodbye.

   - loneliness

i will love you for evermore

Time will fly,
once you stop asking why.
"Why hasn't it happened yet?"
"Why is there, yet another threat?"

Yes, you have learned enough.
And darling, those lessons were only *necessarily tough*.
So as I said, time will fly,
once you stop asking why.

You missed the sunset yesterday,
because you were too busy already overthinking today.
I mean, I love that you are curious
        but you can't know this plan.
So, please try to enjoy the wait as much *as you can.*

I brought you moments of light,
in the hope that you'd be patient whilst I do this fight.
You see, for this blessing to come,
There is a battle that first must be won.

It is not your lesson this time, but theirs instead,
and I am guiding them, *heart and head.*
It's the last hurdle I promise you.
There is not much left to do.

So, please stop asking when, who and why,
and I promise that time will fly.
Because I have got this and I insist,
that what is coming, will not be missed.

      - the universe

Amiee Laura Knubley

i will love you for evermore

Lead a life worthy of your calling.
Be humble and gentle, patient and kind.
Remember to give allowance for each others faults.
Bind with peace and don't let the sun go down on anger.
Give generously and always say *"good"*.
Words can be encouragement.
Live with kindness where you are tender hearted and forgive.
Make the most of opportunity.
These are the words I hope you'll live.

- faiths calling

i will love you for evermore

Dear me,

People aren't always perfect. They don't always do what we need them to do. It sucks and it's ok to be sad about that. It is ok to feel disappointed, angry or whatever it is you feel, but don't stay there, ok? You have to let yourself feel it but it is not a place you can stay.

I know it is temping to keep thinking about why. To replay the scenes in your mind. But just like it is not useful to sit on a chair with a broken leg or stare into a broken mirror, you need to keep moving. It is not useful to stay there.

You've got this big beautiful life to live. So, feel it now, let it out, write it, tell the world, whatever you have to do, but know when it is time. Have a shower, wash it all away and start tomorrow with just a small step. You've got this.

Always,
You.

- *it's ok*

i will love you for evermore

Dear you,

What is love? Love comes in and from so many forms. Love from our family, our friends, a soulmate, our hobbies, our passions, and life. Love to me is life. Love can be so magical and soul fulfilling. Love can fill us with excitement, adventure, anxiety, hope and strength. We go through a life time of love and not all are forever, and that is ok. Some only stay for a while to teach us a lesson - to serve a purpose.

My lesson for you is that you need to experience all the love. It takes courage, but it will fill your soul and teach you the most important thing of all. Faith. Loyalty. Courage. An ability to develop your instincts so that you never sacrifice yourself beyond who you know yourself to be.

When you know and believe your worth you will surround yourself with people who love you unconditionally; so that you can love yourself.

Love yourself first.

Always,
Me.

      - love yourself first

Dear me,

I see you doubting yourself. Limiting your worth based on what society says you should look like, should be doing, should be saying. Why are you still doing that?

It is time. Lets take a deep breath, let it all out. It is time to promise yourself that you will not apologise for your mind. It is full of memories, of ideas and thoughts that matter. You will not apologise for your body. It has carried you to today, it gives you life, and you are not going to question what makes you so beautifully you.

Your heart gave you life even when it was broken. Your legs stood strong even when you didn't think you could move anymore. Your eyes shine in the light and everyday show you moments of magic.

This is your home so don't fill it with shame. This is your home, so speak kind words, and fill it with love, for isn't that how the flowers grow?

You are enough.

You are worthy.

You are loved.

Always,
Me.

- my home

i will love you for evermore

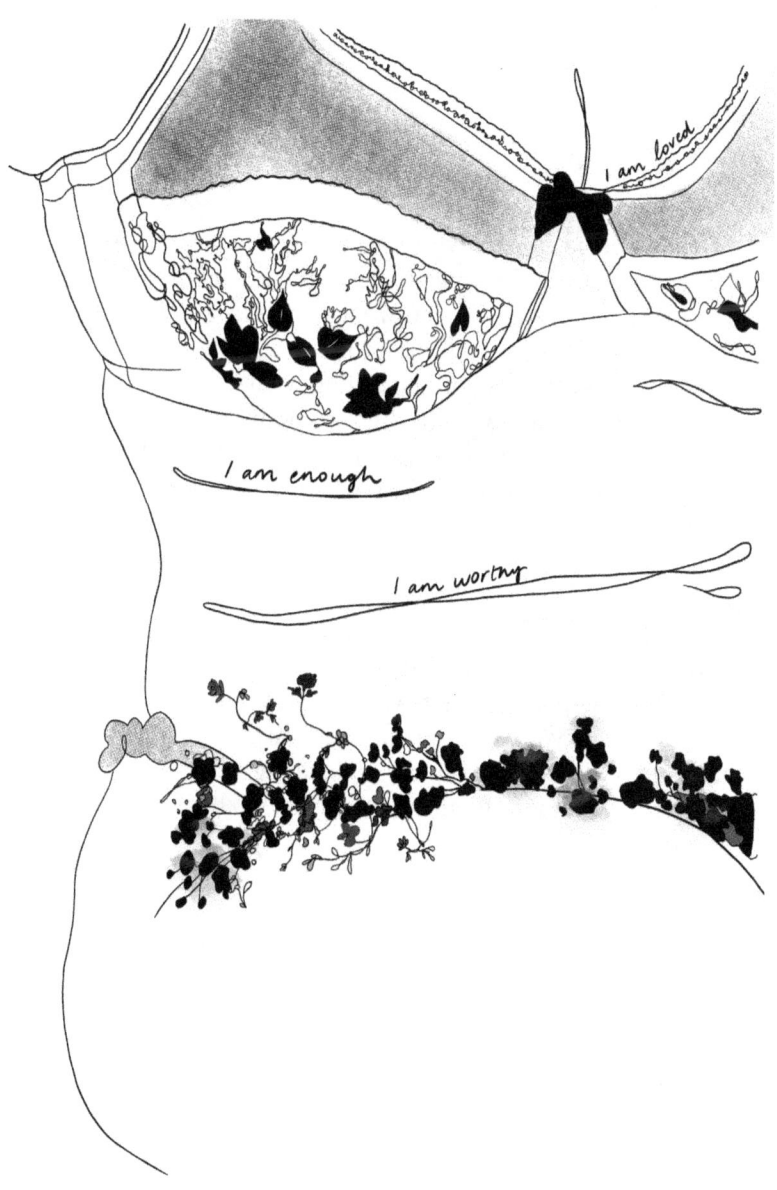

Amiee Laura Knubley

i will love you for evermore

Dear you,

I close my eyes and you ask of me, what now?
I stand firm in my silence but your heart knows.
Live a life worthy of your calling. A purpose that
matches mine. Be humble and gentle even when they
fight. For they do not know,
        how could they?

Darling be patient for we all have faults.
Yours are so big they match the earths existence,
        but don't worry, we will heal together.

Never let the sun set without saying what is on your
heart, for the truth will connect you both.
Not everyone has enough. Life hasn't been as kind
so give when you can and help when you should.
Kindness is always enough.

Your words are magic my dear.
Let me hear them and say them loud.
For it is your voice that will heal.
And only stop when you have done all you can.
    For when you have shown your heart,
said your piece and loved with a love bigger than me,
then my sweet girl, there is nothing else to do
    or to be.

Leave it with me now.

You've done all that you can.

Always,
The Universe.

        - *what now?*

INTUITION

I'm different after knowing.
It is like the sky has opened after a decade
        of it not snowing.
I'm standing under it all.
Each snow flake on my skin, giving me the answers to
        my next fall.

I don't know how it will happen next for me,
but I truly understand the notion now of
    "what will be, will be",
because I survived hell and I rose still.
Our paths are chosen and running like
    the universe's water mill.

In the end it will be ok.
Because between me and the universe
        we will make it that way.
I'm different after knowing this.
    Aren't you? Or are you still afraid that you'll miss?

Amiee Laura Knubley

i will love you for evermore

Tomorrow is not promised to you.
So with that freedom I wonder what it is you will choose to do?

- *blessings*

i will love you for evermore

Dear you,

How long are you going to react?

Yes I know, everyone reacts. But if you're going to stay there and you're going to live in that emotional state, you will see life through that lens of that emotion. The stronger the emotion the more you pay attention, that's where you place your energy.

You're using that circumstance to reaffirm your emotion. That is the response that's has been conditioned. See?

So, how long are you going to react?

Always,
Me.

      -how long?

WAR

Do not mistake peace and quiet for something bad happening.
That is your trauma, the expectation of war speaking.
Just because you grew in chaos,
Lived in pain and survived a great loss,
doesn't mean that is what's coming.
There are no battle sounds humming.

I know you're not used to it,
but please just sit.
Do what you need to calm your mind,
and when you open your eyes, in the quiet you will find,
    moments of joy,
so unexpected you'll whisper *boy, oh boy.*

You see, the sun when she shines,
is never mistaken of the people she finds.
So in him please don't go looking for the war.
His stability will hold you so you can open the door.
I know the quiet can feel a little loud.
You're just used to chaos because that's all that was allowed.

But give it a chance.
Love can be a beautiful romance.
And I promise in time, but only if you let it,
You'll hear the whispers of hope and little bit by little bit,
You'll learn to love yourself
And maybe one day soon you'll leave your amour
    high up on the shelf.

i will love you for evermore

Dear me,

Being alone is hard isn't it? It feels a bit yucky and so very uncomfortable. We aren't built to be solitary creatures, we thrive off connection, belonging. These past couple of years you've been more alone than you've ever been in your whole life.

You've sat in silence that only ever felt deafening. You've lived in moments that only began to feel safe in dreams. You see how, as the survivalist that you are, you turned that uncomfort into peace.

Being alone felt safe.

No one could let you down, walk away or throw words like a knife but you dimmed your light in the process. Only you can let yourself re-enter the world.

You've got the power but my god I hope you choose to shine again. Smile at people when you walk passed, invite a friend for coffee, but please tell me that you will start somewhere.

Always,
You.

- uncomfortable peace

Amiee Laura Knubley

i will love you for evermore

I need help are the hardest words to say.
Especially when you're sat in your darkest day.
You'd think *I was curing cancer,*
or training to be a ballet dancer
But no, *I'm sat here alone.*
Just struggling to pick up the phone.
Hours go by and I haven't moved an inch.
Sometimes my brain stops and I have to give my skin a pinch.
To wake myself up and show I'm still alive.
A reminder that I'm here even if my heart won't revive.

- my broken heart

i will love you for evermore

THE FIGHT

The version of yourself that you became,
got you through the war, *but this love,* this is not the same.

This version of yourself that you had to be,
in order to survive has no place here, *don't you see?*

It is time now to leave that version behind, let it be done.

   That person was for the war, and the war was won.

Amiee Laura Knubley

i will love you for evermore

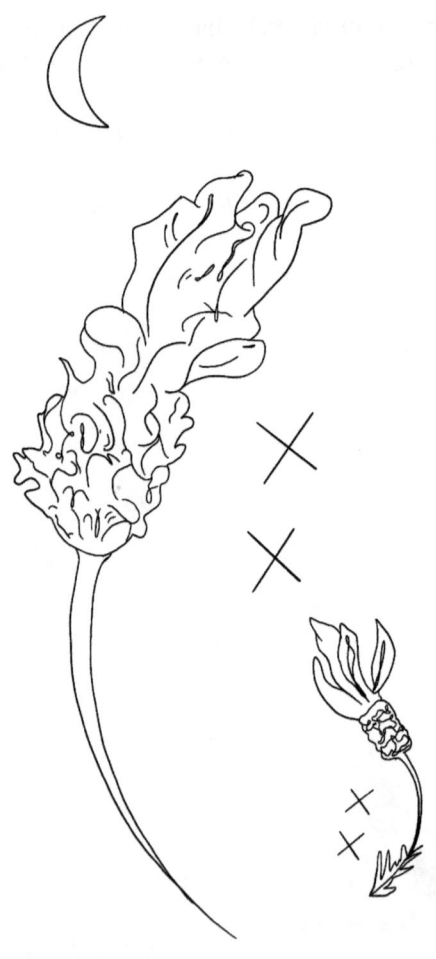

Amiee Laura Knubley

i will love you for evermore

TOO FAR

Have you forgotten who you are?
I did too, and I didn't remember until the road had gone too far.
    Will you listen to me?
And please let me save the you, *the you that you are meant to be.*

You are the bearer of light.
A stable ground who could never tire of this fight.
You are the warrior in this battle we call hope.
Showing the world exactly *how to cope.*

Because you hold a power like no other.
A gentle soul who feels it all, *such a sweet lover.*
A north star guiding each soul away,
from the darkness that can shadow each and every day.

The night sky yields to you.
Your eyes shining the way only the moon can do.
You are made up of all the memories from before.
And every tear you shed washes up on the shore.

If only you would let the river flow through you,
you could use this power to move mountains,
        just like way you are meant to do.
So when you're done sitting in the dark.
Letting the shadows fill you like a hundred acre park.

Remember who you are,
    before the road goes too far.

Amiee Laura Knubley

i will love you for evermore

FOR YOU

You deserve the love you keep trying to give to other people.
Why do you think they deserve more than you,
    like they sit on a steeple?
Let them call you and ask you how you are.
They should see you as their north star.

You deserve flowers on your bed,
and kisses tattooed on your forehead.
You deserve a slow love full of kept promises.
Stable, sure and never any question of what is.

You deserve a love that ever makes you blame yourself and
    never ask the question.
One that fights for you and definitely doesn't see you as a possession.
You deserve a love that always feels like the sun
    as it warms your face.
A home where you will always have a place.

You deserve this love, *for you.*
The one that you give so freely to others, *like it's an easy thing to do.*

Amiee Laura Knubley

i will love you for evermore

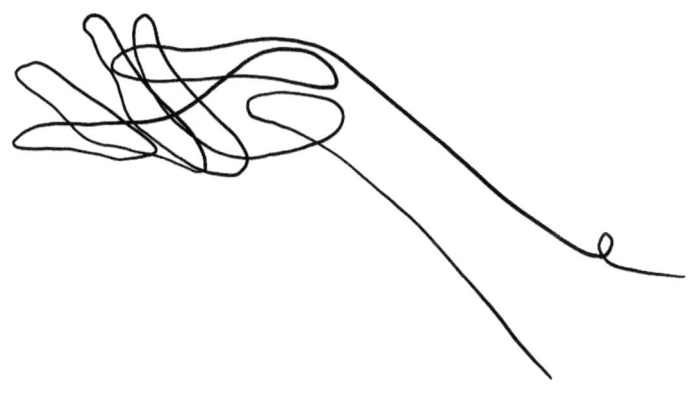

Amiee Laura Knubley

i will love you for evermore

Dear you,

I love all that you are, I love talking with you. I love spending time with you. I love you for everything you have been and everything you are now and everything you will be. I have never doubted that. In the same breath I love all that I am. I love who I have built. I love me too, to my core.

I rebuilt my heart piece by piece and I know now that who I am and what I have to offer is a blessing. I spent my whole twenties begging to be loved. Chasing to show I was worthy. I clawed my way to be seen and in doing so my light was eventually taken. In my naivety I swiftly learned that not every person will be excited by me, they will exist only to take and in reality care little about my existence. So, I stand here now with a promise I made to myself after rebuilding my life. I have promised myself that whilst I can love wholly again, I need to make sure my needs can be met too. I deserve someone to want to and to actually invest in me. I am someone who is worth being excited about and I am allowed to want this. For someone to feel excitement about hearing my voice, seeing my face, watching me grow, excited to hold me and share their life with me.

Somehow I find myself in fleeting moments of uncertainty again because of how you have decided to behave. I am left feeling distance and I am only human so this has me questioning my worth, again. I can't allow that for myself to go on any longer. Now, I know the place you are in and I wish you would let me in. I could carry you until you could walk again, and for forever if that day never came.

i will love you for evermore

I'm here for it all and I've tried to show you that but I can't anymore, *not if I am not chosen*. Not if everyday I can't feel you choosing me too. Never again will I let myself question who I am to someone and what I mean to them; especially when the thought of them takes my breath away. When you can wholly choose me, I will be here. Everything I am will be yours. And if you can't do that, then I wish you nothing but love, and I hope that you can heal to see how worthy and amazing you are.

It is in these moments I will choose to remember that love begins with loving myself. And in our individual journeys of healing and self-acceptance, we will discover the extraordinary power of resilience. Each day is a new opportunity to embrace the brilliance within and to choose a path that leads to the unending light of self love.

Always
Me.

    - i love me too

i will love you for evermore

Dear you,

You are a fighter. A warrior. A goddess, and you don't see your power. You've gone through you life pouring love into other people's cups, until they were overflowing and sometimes to the detriment of yourself; but you knew they needed it. You've been through such a battle and look at you, you have this gold light surrounding you. You haven't let these battles darken your heart, not once did you give up when you fell down and with one foot in front of the other you've come out to the other side shining.

You need to feel proud that you never chose to be a victim. You need to feel proud you took growth over revenge and you need to feel proud that at each point you looked inwards to see how you could do better, how you could evolve and girl, *be proud you always chose kindness.* I know that others don't understand. They chastise you for not shouting from the rooftops and chasing to hurt back but you know you that in your choices you protected your light. You protected your energy and your soul so that upon the other side, it could return to you in tenfolds.

Please don't ever change how you view the world. That is your purpose in this life. You came here to learn this lesson; to show others how to respond and grow in light so that in the next life, you are ready. Others have already learned from you and they will continue to, if you stay the course. You are an inspiration, you are an empathetic healer and you were given this before you were born. You've been separated to realign you on your path and I promise you that you will be ok. Everything will be ok. When you feel lost and doubt this path please re read this message and remind yourself of your light, your love and *what you are destined to give.* Don't worry so much child.

Always,
The Universe.   *- you are everything*

i will love you for evermore

Dear you,

You are worthy of absolutely everything that you desire. I know at somethings you get a little rocked. It is ok. We all do. But I want you to know that you are absolutely magic. There is no one like you and the way you've built your life with passion and hope, *it is awe inspiring.*

Do you know so many people don't get back up after they fall? It's heartbreaking, but that is not you. I won't let it be. *You can't let it be.* So go now, one step in front of the other, just do the next right thing until you can do more, think more, be more. Because that will come, *I promise you.* But for now, take a shower, get outside and have a coffee, call a friend, put on that music. I don't care what it is as long as it gives you a moment of light, because those small steps there? They are the way you fill your life with absolutely everything that you desire.

You beautiful human, the little things matter.

Always,
The Universe.

    - the little things

Amiee Laura Knubley

Dear you,

You are worthy as you are child.

You are whole as you are and everything exists inside of you.

Breathe out what no longer serves you.

You are whole on your own.

Do not say that your voice carries no weight. Your words are being absorbed by the edge of infinity. Today is the last day you are going to cry over this. There is an unshakeable, unimaginable miracle coming that will change everything for you.

You will be in the right places, at the right times. Mark my words child, it's time to move on from the pain, sadness, from the struggle.

The light is coming.

You will feel relief.

If you can move with one piece of advice, let it be this. Let this be the moment you realise that your inner guidance system is your most powerful tool. It is your compass. Follow the compass even if you can't see how you're going to get to where you're going. Follow the compass even when you're standing alone. Follow the compass because I promise it will always bring you home.

Always,
The Universe.

- you are the light

SOULMATE

"What is meant for me will stay".
Those are the words I so clearly hear you say.
That I am on the right path now,
And I must not keep worrying about the details,
           like the how.
I told you that I will follow and I will go like a rivers flow.
But I think when, is all I would like to know.

"What will be, will be".
Those are the words you repeat to me.
But *when, will it be* is all I can think.
I feel like a ship almost about to sink.
Waiting is driving me insane,
and no, I cannot stay here in my lane.

"What is meant for us will not leave".
Hearing you say these things is becoming a pet peeve.
If I have learned all I am meant to,
and there isn't any healing left to do,
then please stop this nonsense,
and stop talking in a future tense.

Amiee Laura Knubley

Dear me,

I am an honour to be with. I love so deeply and I am kind and intelligent. I find magic in the small moments in life. I am intensely loyal and will be there for people important to me, through anything. I am resilient and live my life passionately and unapologetically. But I will not be an option and I will not beg or chase.

My life is planned for a big love, one that chooses me, who would walk through the fire for me. It will be a love that sees the greatness in me and will appreciate the deep love and passion I can bring to their life. They will be kind and generous and inherently curious about people and life.

I will not settle for anything less.

I did not survive hell to have to ask for love. I did not rebuild myself to have someone make me question my worth. I did not find my purpose to fall for anything that falls short of that.

I will be found and when I am, that person will have my heart forever.

Always,
Me.

    - anything less

i will love you for evermore

Amiee Laura Knubley

i will love you for evermore

ENGLISH BAY

I wish I could show you what the ocean does to me.
I can be in complete chaos but I hear the waves
and instead,
      there is serenity.
When I look out I can't take it all in,
and that feels like a reminder
      that I'm not always meant to win.

I am only a small part on this earth, you see.
The ocean reminds me to stop the *'what could be'.*
Instead I am found in the present moment,
the wind brushes my face feeling almost heaven sent.

Maybe in a past life I was a creature of the sea,
because I feel I know the sea's secret, *and it knows me.*
There is a whole world below the surface,
and it connects me to places I would otherwise miss.

When I am stood by the sea, *who I was* isn't so far away.
Connecting me to the history I left on an English bay.
How blessed am I to know such a beautiful place,
and to trust that the sea will always
   wipe the tears from my face.

I leave with a smile and a calm mind each time.
No words can *really* explain why it's my favourite past time.
   But I'm a little more me,
          once I have visited the sea.

Amiee Laura Knubley

i will love you for evermore

NO

In the cold light of day,
can you find the words to say?
I can't.

In the warmth of night,
do you have peace or what you called, the fight?
I don't.

In the depths of your voice, do you know the prayer?
Because I don't think it sounds very fair.
I know.

Roar like the thunder and show me your fire.
There is no other way to call out the liar.
I see.

It is time for a new day so ignore the whispers and everything that they will say.
Your words will heal and your eyes will light the way.
I promise.

That is enough.
You don't need to be so tough.
I cry.

Amiee Laura Knubley

i will love you for evermore

In her ability to create light,
the moon doesn't question her place at night.
For she knows that is where she shines best.
She is not tagging along like an uninvited guest.

The moon shines like the main event,
because she never questioned what they meant,
when they gave her a purpose to shine.
She just began promising *"I will make the sky mine"*.

    - self belief

i will love you for evermore

Amiee Laura Knubley

i will love you for evermore

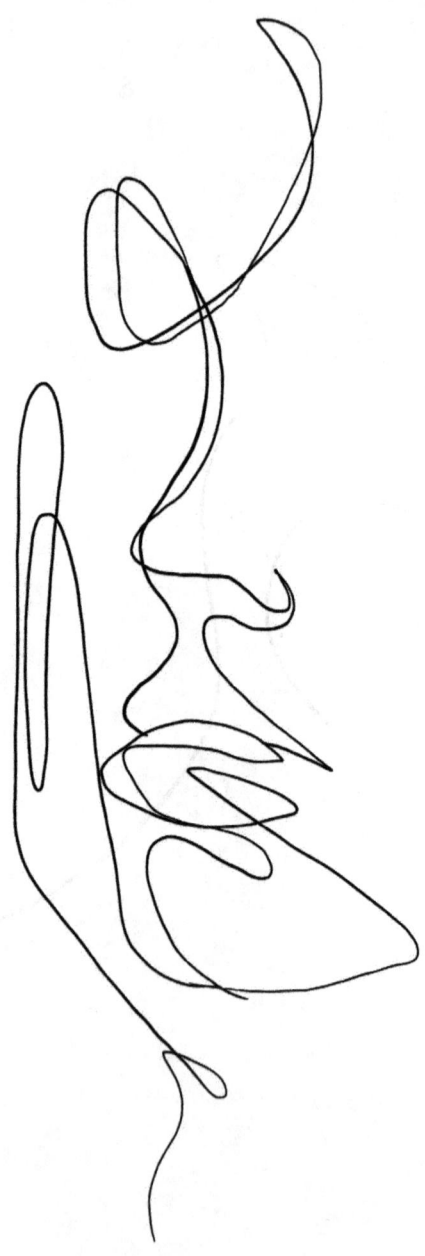

Amiee Laura Knubley

i will love you for evermore

HEALER

Its not always easy being you, *a beautiful healing empath.*
Your light surrounds you, always providing a path.
I see your tired eyes and how you question your existence.
It is like you try to create protection with your distance.

But the sun doesn't help the flowers grow by *hiding.*
And the moon doesn't move the seas by never deciding.
They shine their light.
Every day, and every night.

They trust their purpose and what they're here to do.
So my darling, why is it that you struggle to do this too.
When you hide away people notice
        the light is missing from their day.

Please don't roll your eyes at me like I'm speaking in cliches.

I see you sitting in your doubt.
Ignoring the signs like you don't know what they're about.
It is time to stand proud because *you know, who you are.*
The world has been crying for their north star.

So, give them your light.
And please remind them how to win the fight.

Amiee Laura Knubley

i will love you for evermore

- END -

Dear you,

As we come to the end of this poetic journey through the pages of *"Evermore,"* I want to take a moment in one last letter, as I bodly hope I can call us friends, family even? For that is where true vulnerability grows, is it not? These words, these verses, they are more than ink on paper. They are the echoes of my soul and the whispers of my journey. I hope you heard yourself in these words as you read. My heart will be smiling if you have written in the margins and highlighted when your heart felt what it needed to.

As you know, through these words, I've shared my journey through self-discovery, love, infertility, loss, grief, separation, and heartbreak. But I've also embraced and celebrated the transformative power of true love, motherhood, friendship, and self-acceptance. I hope you agree now, these moments in life are truly magic, aren't they?

Love, in all its forms, is the thread that weaves through, not just the tapestry of *"Evermore"*, but in reality - in both our lives. Love that may have led to pain but has also been the crucible for strength, resilience, and unexplainable joy. It's these moments of inexplicable bliss that our souls crave— moments when we are truly alive.

As you've journeyed through these pages, I hope you've discovered pieces of yourself, resonating with the words that may have felt like your own unspoken truths. I encourage you to be courageous, to find your voice, and to share your unique experience, for it is through vulnerability that we connect with the light that is always present.

These moments in *"Evermore"* haven't defined me, they are just a part of me, and so for you now, remember that no situation, no heartache, no joy, soley defines you. Your worth is intrinsic, a light within that shines brightly, regardless of life's twists and turns.

What you do matters, and you are loved, more than you can fathom. You are enough, just as you are, with all your beautifully imperfect, raw, and messy truth.

So, dear reader, as you conclude this chapter, remember that every ending is but a prelude to a new beginning. Choose to embark on your healing journey, to express yourself bravely, and to know that you are never alone. There is always light in the darkness, and within you, that light shines eternally.

Embrace the courage to live life boldly, for every day is a choice—a choice to feel, to heal, and to thrive. Life is a journey of embracing the light within, and in doing so, we create our own story, one of strength, resilience, and unceasing hope.

As a practical step on your healing journey, I encourage you to embrace the power of self-expression through journaling. Pick a couple of key poems or letters if you need a guide but allow your thoughts, feelings, and experiences to flow onto the next few empty pages. Then in the pages of your own journal, you'll discover a safe space to explore your innermost thoughts and emotions. This practice can be a profound companion on your path to healing.

I wish you nothing but love, and the courage to step into your power boldy.

All my love,
Always, forever, for evermore.
Amiee

Journal

Journal

Journal

www.ingramcontent.com/pod-product-compliance
Lightning Source LLC
Chambersburg PA
CBHW072046160426
43197CB00014B/2650